Existential Dragons

A guide for mental health therapists that would like to use Dungeons & Dragons or other role-playing games as a group therapy tool

Ryan Scott, LMHC and Beverly Hoberg, LPC

"My girls have been through a lot in the past several years. They've seen five different therapists, and they've been in too many groups to count, but until the Dungeons & Dragons group, I never really noticed all that much change. I mean they stopped yelling and hitting each other and that sort of thing, but as far as self-confidence and independent thinking, I honestly think that it's the D&D group that did it. I know that now they are getting along and they have all of these inside jokes about Gnomes, and Wizards…. I know it's that group that has opened them up. They leave the house and see friends now. They're happy! I can't say enough about that group, and you can tell everyone I said so!" ~ Human mother

Dedication

To the kids that helped us learn about this process.

May the dice be ever in your favor.

Ryan and Bev

Foreword

Once upon a time, in a land filled with many monsters and no heroes, a teenage boy walked into his therapist's room and described an adventure that he had that changed how he thought about himself. The boy had been fearful of pretty much everything in his life and had gotten the chance to be a cleric for one night in a game of Dungeons & Dragons. Though he did not know it, this was the beginning of successful socialization for this boy. He described how he was a valuable member of the team and had felt friendship and comradery from his teammates, which was something that had previously been missing in his life. This type of epic physical adventure is something that the boy would never have been able to experience anywhere else, due to not only his depression, and almost debilitating social anxiety, but due to his multiple physical complications from birth. This was the day that his therapist walked down the hall and asked another therapist if he knew how to play Dungeons & Dragons.

In a move that could have been written in a script for a Dungeons & Dragons campaign, the second therapist immediately smiled and said that he had just talked to another person about that same idea. This is the day that Ryan and Bev formed their first Dungeons & Dragons based therapy group.

This book was written for therapists that would like to explore the possibility of using Dungeons & Dragons for their clients in need. If you are reading this book right now, then chances are that you are a therapist looking for a new way to help clients through social anxiety, depression and more. We hope that you enjoy the book and that you find it useful. Life after all, is an epic adventure.

PREFACE

Role-playing games (RPGs), such as Dungeons & Dragons, are becoming an increasingly popular therapeutic tool among mental health professionals, and a corresponding increase in research journal articles have been written about the efficacy in such settings. However, before this book, there was a stark lack of literature that addressed the logistics of using RPG's as part of mental health therapy groups. This work will focus on using Dungeons & Dragons (D&D), as it is an archetypical and commonly-available RPG. The authors of this book felt that it was time to make a book available for therapists, counselors, psychologists, social workers, and psychiatrists that work with groups of individuals. D&D has gone through many iterations over the years and is currently on its fifth edition, though all share common themes of adventure and storytelling.

We hope that this text will serve as an impetus for other groups to follow. This book is broken down into several factors and is meant to guide a potential provider or facilitator from the beginning, assuming no base knowledge of D&D. Although the emphasis of this book is related to social factors - developing social skills and reducing social anxiety - it includes a foundation for understanding and working with a variety of individuals, contexts, and diagnoses.

Quotes from past and present group members are scattered throughout the book, giving a glimpse into the thoughts and feelings that arise in the books. All quotes were chosen because they were unidentifiable as to maintain client confidentiality and attributed to their RPG persona. All quotes were approved beforehand by the client and, where appropriate, the clients' families.

All case studies have been written with permission by clients and their families and are also written in a way that conceals their identities.

Dutch Knight from the 13th century.

Acknowledgments

Thank you to Wizards of the Coast for giving us permission to use references to, and images of, their Dungeons & Dragons material.

A very special thank you to the kids and parents that gave their quotes to the book.

Belon's dragon, dated 1588.

Contents

Chapter 1   Introduction to the World of Dungeons & Dragons

      How we got started

      What is existentialism?

      What is shared storytelling?

      What is the Hero's Journey

      What are Role Playing Games?

      What is Dungeons & Dragons?

Chapter 2   Empirical Evidence and Research

      So this is fun, but how is this therapeutic?

      How a therapist as a DM can change minds and hearts

Chapter 3   Before the first working session

      Three paths to choose from

      Packaged adventures

      Backstories

      Adding therapeutic content

        The Hero's Journey

        Useful monsters

        Non-player characters

        Maps, puzzles, contests, and other things that will make you think

        Stacking your therapeutic deck

        Going with the flow when clients do not

        Writing therapeutic storylines

        Building non-player characters

        The magic is inside the client

        Clients don't die in therapy

        The importance of having a headquarters

        The "problem" player

        Learning the game

Chapter 4   Setting up the first session

        Choosing character class

        Opportunity and challenges with each class

        Choosing character race

        Choosing character alignment

        Filling out character sheets

        A few pre-session rules (they're more like guidelines really)

        Supplies that you will need

        Understanding the basic rules of the game (the real ones)

Chapter 5   First game session and beyond

        The first session

        Common issues that arise

        Examples of a storyline

        Group conflicts

        Timing your ending (watching the clock)

Chapter 6   Thoughts about interventions by diagnosis

        About diagnosis in general

        Social Anxiety

        PTSD and Trauma

        Adjustment Disorders

        Depression, Dysthymia, and Mood Disorders

        Asperger's and Autism and Spectrum Disorders

        Attention Deficit Hyperactivity Disorder and Attention Deficit Disorder

        Talented and Gifted

        Electronic Addiction

Chapter 7		Wisdom points earned (case studies and practical examples)
		The Case of the Red Dragon (Overcoming trauma)
		Orville Redenbacher (Cheating yourself)
		The Drow (changing your world)
		The Fighter (when other people give you a label)
		Dwarven Beverages (Teenagers and alcohol)
		The Sisiutl (Knowing your worth)
		The Airship Pirate (Domestic violence and its effect on children)
Chapter 8		Worksheets and handouts
		Welcome to the Library
		Bardic Poetry
		I Am From
		I Am
		Question forms (and pre and post questionnaires)

References

"I'm in a good mood for at least two days after our group. This group is different. Very different. I think it works because you have a different way of expressing yourself and even different feelings. You can meet new people in a non-scary way, and people that you probably wouldn't know any other way and they are kind of similar to you, which feels really good. You can be brave or cowardly as you really feel and no one will judge you about it. There are all kinds of feelings that I can explore and it's safe, and exploring all of those feelings, it kind of raises your mood. I've been in therapy for a long time, and in a bunch of therapy groups, and therapy is good and groups are good and all, well sometimes, but this is different. I can feel the difference. This is me." ~ Elf Bard (age 15)

CHAPTER 1

Introduction to the world of Dungeons & Dragons

How we got started

In the spring of 2015, two therapists in Springfield, Oregon, were talking about groups to help teenagers with social anxieties. By coincidence, one of the therapists mentioned that a 14-year-old client had played a Dungeons & Dragons game and it raised his mood and his understanding of things around him while the other therapist mentioned that he had spoken to an adult client that had the same experiences playing the game. They decided that further research was needed. The therapists explored media and found a podcast of a therapy group for teenage boys that sounded intriguing, and they talked to several others that had played the game in high school and college and had found some social success. Exploring journal studies came next, and the benefits for mental health began to shine. After presenting it to administrators at the non-profit that the therapists worked at, an Existential Therapy and Shared Storytelling group using Dungeons & Dragons was born.

The group has had excellent success with teenage and pre-teenage clients with social anxiety, depression, attention issues, trauma, and more. One of the benefits of using an established role playing game as a therapeutic tool is that after the group is over, clients frequently begin their own games outside of therapy, which helps them form (or join) a social group of their own. Dungeons & Dragons has upwards of 20 million estimated players alone. Since D&D is so ubiquitous and includes player settings including college campuses, game stores, conventions, and organized meet-ups, the chance to find a social group is high, regardless of where a person may be. It is a powerful tool for social anxiety, especially for those with preexisting interests in role-playing games. This group, as it developed, was built on the foundations of Existential Therapy, Shared Storytelling, and Joseph Campbell's Hero's Journey.

What is Existentialism?

Existentialism is a philosophical theory that emphasizes the existence of the individual person as a free and responsible agent, capable of determining their own development through acts of the will. The word existentialism comes from the Danish language, and means "condition of existence." Existentialism stems directly from the work of philosophers through their intellectual and literary movements.

Although there are several different existential schools of thought, this section will be focusing primarily on the Sartrean and Gestalten theories of existentialism. Both of these theoretical perspectives focus on the balance between the freedom of choice that we have as humans and the responsibility that comes with that freedom.

The Sartrean perspective is generally less concerned with a person's past and more concerned with the choices that are available to them in the present and the future. Within the Sartrean teachings, an individual may choose to reflect upon how they have responded to challenges in the past, but the attention ultimately shifts to new responses that are available at the moment. From Sartre's perspective, complete freedom leads to complete responsibility, which creates anxiety. In order to avoid this anxiety, we must learn to find a balance between freedom and responsibility.

Gestalt therapy is a phenomenological-existential therapy that is designed to help enlighten individuals whose preexisting attitudes do not line up with their deeper beliefs. Its goal is for clients to become aware of what they are doing, how they are doing it, and how they can change themselves while simultaneously learning to accept and value themselves. The emphasis during the Gestalt therapeutic process is on what is being done, the thought, and feeling in the moment.

The most common use of existentialism in therapy is to provide a philosophy that serves as a base to help an individual understand the core elements of their life, with a focus on the present and the future. By gaining insight into the limitations of being human, it is then possible to develop coping skills to reduce distress that comes from living within these boundaries. Through existentialism, it is possible for people to find life satisfaction and meaning in their lives by becoming more courageous and confident with their choices.

What is Shared Storytelling?

Shared storytelling refers to the practice of sharing narratives with others. From a theoretical therapeutic perspective, shared storytelling is a communication tool that is used to organize and interpret both individual phenomena and larger events. From the moment a story is selected for sharing with others, its existence becomes vulnerable to the ideals of right and wrong, true or false, worth or worthlessness. Shared storytelling helps to foster a sense of group unity and community and also helps to define the framework of moral propriety and decorum within a group and within each individual member of that group. In a therapeutic group setting, shared storytelling creates a tool by which group members work collaboratively to further their story. Therapeutic shared storytelling is a method of producing insight, correcting a cognitive distortion, or providing an outlet for anxiety in a socially acceptable manner.

What is the Hero's Journey?

The Hero's Journey (a.k.a. the "Monomyth") is a template for tales that have been told for thousands of years and outlines the human desire to change and grow. In the beginning of the journey, the hero (in our case, the client) starts out in a place or a situation that they want to change and goes through a transformation from the place of discomfort into a place of self-understanding. Since the Hero's Journey will take a bit of time to explain, the author's have included a larger section about it later in the book.

What are role playing games?

A role-playing game (RPG) is a game in which a player takes on the persona of a character, becoming responsible for their decisions, interactions, and choices. There are many forms of RPG's, from simple and informal (e.g., two children playing house) to highly complex and formal (e.g., two spouses changing respective roles as a couple's counseling exercise). In both examples, role playing is used to facilitate building of skills, such as learning task performance or developing empathy and perspective. Role playing frequently also finds a home in therapeutic settings, specifically cognitive-behavioral therapy, where clients may practice situations with their therapist or a group in order to build skills when similar situations are encountered in daily life. For example, a client with depressive symptoms may be asked to describe positives about themselves from an outsider's perspective, taking on a third-person role in order to build skills.

What is Dungeons & Dragons?

Dungeons & Dragons is a role-playing game (often referred to as D&D) and is a major influence on modern RPG's. It was designed by Gary Gygax and Dave Arneson and bears many similarities to world mythology and history, as well as contemporary fantasy novels as such as J.R.R. Tolkien's The Lord of the Rings and The Hobbit. Dungeons & Dragons is currently in its 5th edition, released in 2014, and is published by Wizards of the Coast (now a subsidiary of Hasbro).

A large benefit of Dungeons & Dragons it that it can be played anywhere, but traditionally takes place around a table and uses the imagination of the players to further the gameplay. Each player in the game creates a character (or characters) as their avatar(s). These characters embark on an adventure into a fantasy setting through the guidance of the game leader, called a Dungeon Master (DM) or Game Master (GM). Dungeons & Dragons games often are small groups, having between three and eight players that interact together while on an overarching campaign or plotline (e.g., to save a land from a dragon or to bring peace to warring families). Characters often interact with non-player characters (NPC's) which are controlled by the person running the game - the Dungeon Master - such as monsters, townsfolk, and antagonists. Dungeons & Dragons by nature employs a variety of social rules, cognitive skills, decision making tasks, stress management and focus-oriented situations. Dungeons & Dragons players must use logic, basic mathematics, and above all, imagination during the game to achieve their goals.

Wyvern Dragon, circa 1347

"Just because you grew up in a house full of monsters, doesn't mean that you have to be one." ~ Drow Wizard, age 13

Chapter 2

Empirical Evidence and Research

So this looks fun, but how is it therapeutic?

So about now, we are guessing that therapists are asking themselves, "So this looks like fun, but how is it therapeutic?" The authors asked themselves the same thing when they first started looking into the benefits of role-playing games. We hit the research journals (as therapists do), and decided to add this chapter as an easy resource for other professionals or curious minds that would like to know more about the empirical evidence. Where possible, the specific RPG of Dungeons & Dragons has been chosen over others (from the wide variety of role-playing games). This chapter by no means contains all of the empirical evidence that is available, but only the articles that the authors felt were most informative to therapists considering this modality.

When reviewing the literature about role-playing games, three main emerging themes became evident:

1. Role-playing provides an avenue to experience social interaction without the typical social pressure that accompanies other social activities.

2. Role-playing increases a client's sense of personal control and efficacy.

3. Role-playing increases a client's social skills, leading to a report in life satisfaction.

These themes are also the themes that the authors found with their own clients when we began to use Dungeons & Dragons as a therapeutic intervention. Looking at the history of role-playing games, they have existed as long as humans have been in existence interacting with each other. It seems safe to say that there are rarely children that have not played in imaginary roles, being kings and queens, a super spy or warrior protector. Such games satisfy the mental health needs of young humans on many levels: children play games to explore social roles, expand social skills, examine possible futures, and polish communication skills. Role-playing in the form of play-therapy games have shown to be beneficial in teaching children the self-concept, behavioral changes, cognitive abilities, social skills, and anxiety management that is needed to maintain a healthy self (Bratton & Ray, 2000). In the same fashion as childhood play, Dungeons & Dragons has made a natural transition from childhood learning into the psychoeducation of a modern therapy session.

The impact of role-playing games is a particularly important part of adolescent growth and a fundamental maturational task (Allison, von Wahlde, Shockley, Gabbard 2006). Further studies show that stress, helplessness, social introversion, and low-self esteem that contribute to depressive symptoms may be relieved by the use of role-playing games (Kaiser and Berndt, et.al). Similarly, poor self-concept is a primary concern for gifted students that are having difficulty relating to their social arena (Kaiser and Berndt, 2004). The concept of fantasy that is found in role-playing games offers adolescents the opportunity to engage in extended childhood role playing, without the complicating factor of making them feel as if still young children or participating in "childish" games. In the case of group therapy that uses role-playing games as a base for its sessions, the resistant teenager may see the opportunity to take place in what is viewed as a leisurely activity with others; as such, they may be willing to come to sessions and participate in therapy more easily, where they would have otherwise refused to participate.

A number of clinical case studies and researchers have examined therapeutic uses for fantasy role-playing and observed that the participants often put their own personalities into their characters (Waskul and Lust, 2004, Bersier, 2006; Enfield, 2007; Hitchen & Drachen, 2009). This temporary transference of self helps participants to establish a sense of self-representation and control (Krout & Tabin 2005). In cases where a therapist guided the game play and asked the players to play out the strengths or weaknesses of their characters, an increase in self understanding and emotional maturity was founded (Bersier, 2006; Enfield, 2007; Hitchens & Drachen, 2009).

In journal literature, some of the most interesting articles have been ones that include case studies. One of the earliest and most striking was penned in 1994 by a psychiatrist that was working with a 19-year-old Caucasian male with schizoid personality tendencies. The teenager began to see the psychiatrist after a serious attempt at suicide. Through the therapeutic conversation with the psychiatrist, it was discovered that the teenager had a brother with severe mental delays and his patient deeply resented the constant attention that was given to the brother. The teenager stated to his psychiatrist that his parents made him feel rejected and criticized him for being angry or envious of his brother and being left with a feeling that, "There was something wrong with me for having these feelings." The teenager dropped out of school and was left with no friends, no social contacts, and inadequate social skills to understand how to seek out relationships. After the suicide attempt, the teenager and his psychiatrist arranged for the him to begin a therapeutic Dungeons & Dragons group. Within a few weeks of the group's beginning, the teenager began to talk about the game in his therapy sessions and returned to school. The teenager stated that, during the game, he had been able to experience a full range of feelings (i.e., hate to love). With the tolerant and encouraging attitude of his psychiatrist, the patient developed the sense that these emotions were permissible and that he had mastery over them (Blackmon,1994).

In 2000, a 14-year-old Native American boy with diabetes was hospitalized due to ketoacidosis (a buildup of ketones - blood acids - that result in a dangerous change to body pH). The boy had been removed from his parents care on the grounds of parental neglect and had since lived in several foster homes. The Department of Social Services recommended psychiatric intervention due to depression, acting out, and refusal to cooperate with authority figures. The assigned psychiatrist attempted art therapy projects, but as soon as the boy figured out that he was not attending an art class, he refused to cooperate with therapy any further. The psychiatrist attempted talking to the boy about Dungeons & Dragons, and doing so allowed them to finally make a connection. The psychiatrist reports, "The only time he smiled was when he was discussing the game Dungeons & Dragons." The psychiatrist did not play the actual game with the client, but used the imagery from the game to help the client visualize the possibilities in his life and make changes that he needed to make. The psychiatrist concluded, "I realized that silence can be as effective as speaking, and that one needs to be open-minded about the tactics and techniques employed."

Role-playing can be seen as a take on psychodrama that offers an exceptional tool for therapists to connect to teenagers, particularly teenagers that are resistant to coming to therapy. Psychodrama and role-playing, in the form of a Dungeons & Dragons therapy group, also offers a unique chance for therapists to expand their therapeutic tool box and offer their clients the opportunity to act - either as themselves or to experience a new and unfamiliar role - along with new and even life-changing thoughts and ideas, all within a safe and controlled environment.

This therapy modality can be a way to learn to reduce social fears, increase social skills, navigate complex social interactions, and create a sense of belonging that is difficult for many clients. In short, Dungeons & Dragons is a great way to for clients to gain insight into themselves, and others.

As a final note, the authors of this book strongly recommend that a client who participates in a Dungeons & Dragons therapy group also process the group regularly with his or her own individual therapist. It should go without saying that it is beneficial for the client to have a therapist that is understanding to the value of psychodrama and role-playing.

How a therapist as DM can change minds and hearts

If you have ever played Dungeons & Dragons before, you have likely heard the DM referred to as, "The one that makes the world," or, more comically, "The one the one that does all the work." While there are varying thoughts about the extent of the role of DM, they serve a highly important core purpose: the DM sets the mood for the game and is the primary designer of the world in which the characters will traverse. The situations and challenges that the DM gives to the adventurers create the experience for the clients. That means that almost everything that happens in the game can be mediated, if not fully controlled, by the therapist-turned-DM. It is important to know this because, as those who have run groups may have experienced, there will be some clients that will need a soft touch, special attention, or even a challenge with the end goal of keeping all clients happy and moving forward in their therapeutic goals at the same time. To do so successfully means that the DM-therapist is the most powerful and final line of defense to create and maintain a fair and enjoyable group experience.

In our own experiences in using Dungeons & Dragons in a therapy group setting, we have found that limiting the number of players to 6-8 allows each player to have plenty of time to react to the situations that are being presented without leaving out group members. Each therapist will have to decide the number that is right for their group members, but it is suggested by the authors that group size be carefully monitored based on staffing, clients, group dynamics, and type/severity of symptoms. This allows for the DM-therapist to address each group member individually as needed, and allows the best possible chance for each group member to interact with other group members in a therapeutic manner. Limiting group sizes also minimizes the risk for negative interactions between characters.

"If it wasn't for this group, I wouldn't be social at all. I'd kind of given up on people. Being part of this group is probably the smartest thing that I have ever done before. I'm learning to socialize again." Half-Elf Ranger (age 14)

CHAPTER 3

Before the first working session

Three paths to choose from

There are three broad types of RPG play categories available to therapists. These three types of games have various names, but we prefer the terms "Theater of the Mind," "Miniatures and Props," and "Cosplay Adventures."

- Theater of the Mind refers to playing the game without the use of tabletop props or miniatures, or with very limited visual aides, and occasionally with a grid or map that can be used for clarity's sake. This technique appears to encourage the most imagination and works well for teenagers or those less in need of visual or tactical stimulation. Theater of the Mind also adds the extra requirement that a DM-therapist needs to be an excellent story-seller because the group has few visuals to rely on during the sessions. Both therapists and group members can benefit from the increased freedom of movement and expression that Theater of the Mind grants during the session. The downside of this technique is that it leaves more room for error; without physical items to look at, players can get lost, misunderstand each other's intentions or actions, or make incorrect assumptions about situations as they are encountered.

- Miniatures and Props refers to the use of physical miniature characters and/or terrain that are placed on tabletop or electronic grids. The sophistication of the props can vary from simple tokens (e.g., coins or board game pieces) to elaborate and scale-size environments made of cardboard or foam. This type of game play appears to be helpful to younger teens by providing a supplemental structure to the story, but limits the game play somewhat because the characters can only choose to move within the limits of the grids that have been laid out. Dungeons & Dragons handbooks include rules and examples for grid play, as it allows for convenient measuring of speeds, distances, areas, and allows characters to make decisions based on this hard-and-fast data. Creating the board and props can take a large amount of time and planning on part of the DM, but can be reused over time and groups.
- Cosplay Adventures, refers to the type of play that most of us experienced as a child, and can be the most encompassing and engrossing. Clients can dress as their character and physically interact with each other as their character would, as if in a theatre play. One downfall of Cosplay Adventures is the demand for logistics: a large space is needed for game play, and the price of costumes and props can escalate. This type of play may also be met with resistance by clients

and labeled as "silly" or "too time intensive." Conversely, too much focus on focus on the logistics can become distracting away from the therapeutic content.

Packaged adventures

For beginning DM-therapist, or for DM-therapists needing a boost for creative story ideas, Wizards of the Coast has pre-boxed adventures available. These ready-made adventures come with everything that you need to pull off an exciting Theater of the Mind (and more!) adventure and can be easily adapted to meet the needs of a Miniature and Props or a Cosplay Adventure. One favorite is "Dungeons & Dragons Starter Set - Subterranean Labyrinth." The therapeutic content is easily added to this starter set, because it includes opportunities for the group to work together while sharing ideas about how values guide their behavior, as well as reinforcing that our past experiences guide our current decisions, and how our decisions help us reach our goals. Friendship and social skills are built into most Dungeons & Dragons adventures by nature of the setting and this one includes it, plus a few opportunities to discuss family dynamics and loyalty to self and others. Prepackaged adventures can be found at any good "gaming store" or online.

Backstories

Before the adventure part of the session begins, therapists should have a portion of the first session that is set aside so that the client can create a character that he or she wants to work with. This is also a time to ask the client if they would like to write a backstory for their character. A backstory tells where the character came from and any significant experiences that he or she might have had that would affect the way that the character navigates through the world. They can be highly complex or very simple, depending on the writer's preference and ability. Alternatively, clients can be assigned a backstory as homework for the next session.

A note to therapists: pay close attention to your clients' backstories. These have proven to be a wealth of information about the client themselves and their own perspectives on the world. Backstories are often written from the their personal experiences and placed into the game.

Adding therapeutic content

Therapists new to Dungeons & Dragons may want to start out using prepared adventures, then add therapeutic content to the game to guide their clients to where the client would like to be; however, therapists with background experience or wanting to tailor their approach will benefit from writing their own adventures. Therapists that write their own adventures will be able to tailor the adventures to match more of their client's real life. Information for writing your own adventure lines can be gained by speaking to the individual group members parents or therapists. An example of this might be if a client is having trouble with social skills, some extra down time for the characters can be written in.

The D&D Player's Handbook says that D&D has three major pillars of gameplay: Exploration, Interaction, and Combat. Each client will be choosing a race, a class, and an alignment for their character. The trick for the DM therapist is to combine all of these things so that each player's character is involved in a way that the client benefits from the session. Writing an adventure for this will probably seem more daunting than it will actually be since therapeutic content during an epic adventure will happen, no matter what the DM writes (within reason of course). If the adventure is thought of as an outing (e.g., school outing, family outing) the chance to interact with others is available, it just needs to be noticed. Just being together and socializing will help clients who are struggling to learn workable social skills. Clients that are having a hard time relating to others will have the opportunity to experiment with new modes of relating to others. Clients can explore what they want to learn more about in a safe and creative environment with boundaries that are guided by the therapist and the other group members. The game itself will help give the therapist the platform to explore many aspects of the clients thought process and feelings that would not be normally available in an individual session in an office.

Some suggestions are:

- A client that is having trouble being respectful to adults might meet a wise elder along the journey that will be a guide for his character, provided that he is respectful.
- A client that is afraid of spiders might meet a talking spider that has a clue to a riddle.
- A client that is angry at his parents may have his character come across an wise old person with some enlightening words of wisdom.

- A client that is anxious about being in a new foster home might visit the homes of the elves and learn about the orphans they took in after the great dragon attack.

Whatever the client is going through, it can be written into the story plot. A suggestion is to be subtle with adding therapeutic content to the story lines. Later in the book, there are some examples of story lines that worked well. Not all of the story lines were written that way. Role playing games, by nature, evolve as the group members want it to, so as the therapist, just be prepared to go with the flow.

Ideas for adding therapeutic content are often richer when the client's individual therapist and parents (when appropriate) are involved. One example is that during one session, a sibling set had been arguing at home. The mother reported that this had been going on for a month and it was eating away at the peacefulness of the household. The DM-therapists wrote an adventure where the two siblings would have to rely on each other to get across a dangerous ice lake. This took a turn where the siblings (and the other adventurers) would have been separated if they could not answer a question posed by a dragon, about how they were valuable to each other. In order to continue with their beloved adventure, the siblings had to recall times in their lives when they supported each other. This was probably one of the most powerful sessions that we had and the entire group of teenagers was in tears. The mother reported that the something changed that night, and the siblings stopped their fighting, and kept referring to "the ice lake dragon."

One trick to keeping clients happy during sessions is to include things from their lives and the lives of their character without being overly blunt. (e.g., a boy that has had an unpleasant interaction with a girl at school might find a non-player character girl that he can try to replay the scene and figure out what went wrong). A typical quest can easily be based around teachable moments or moments that present with distress due to mental health-related symptoms.

The Hero's Journey

As referenced earlier in the book, the Hero's Journey is a template that can be used to help organize your adventure. The Hero's Journey has three main sections to it which are broken down into seventeen smaller parts.

The three main sections are:

1. Departure from the normal world
2. Initiation into the unknown world
3. Return to the normal world

The seventeen smaller parts are:

1. The call to adventure
2. Refusal of the call
3. Supernatural aid
4. Crossing the threshold
5. Belly of the whale
6. The road of trials
7. Meeting with the Goddess

8. The temptress

9. Atonement with the father

10. Apotheosis

11. The ultimate boon

12. Refusal of the return

13. The magic flight

14. Rescue from without

15. Crossing the return threshold

16. Master of two worlds

17. Freedom to live

In the normal world, the hero (the individual client, even though they will be working as a group) feels that he or she is not truly happy where they are. In the real world, the client could be in detention, a stressful foster home, a school that they don't feel appreciated in, or any number of situations where the client feels that they are not fully happy. If possible, it is can be helpful to directly suggest to the client that they write their backstory to include a storyline that is abstractly similar to their own life, without it being obviously their real life (and only if the client is comfortable doing so). This will engage the client deeper in the story to come. For example, if a client was in detention, then their starting out by being a prisoner in an Orc prison might be a good option; if a client is in a foster home, then a backstory about being in an rouge-run orphanage might be an option. Of course, in the end it is always up to the client to write their backstory.

The following part of the Hero's Journey involves their character somehow learning about a different way of life. This might be a good time to reflect on who told them about the new way of life - is this a trusted person? Is the information a bit dodgy? In the end, the idea is for the client to learn to figure out how to make good decisions based on solid information.

The next part of the Hero's Journey is whether the client's character will refuse the call to investigate the new world or the new way of thinking. If the client refuses, then nothing changes for him and he remains in his normal world, doing what he has always done, but typically there is a pressure to change that will happen and encourage movement. For example, the character will keep having dreams of a better world or will have some other increase in uncomfortableness until the character chooses to be brave and try the adventure (this is not really a common problem in the Dungeons & Dragons therapy groups itself, as the clients have all entered the room knowing that they are there to have an adventure, but this step is a good one to talk about after the game part of the therapy session has finished).

Once the client/character has crossed the threshold, a series of trials and failures can happen, depending on the needs of the client/characters in the group. These adventures can be built using information from the clients or the client's parents, and will most likely change from week to week, depending on the client's current situations. For example, if one week the client is fighting with her brother, then that alliance can be strengthened by having them work on a magical puzzle together, or to find themselves alone at the end of town and needing the help of one another to get back to the group.

After the client has entered into the unknown world, they will most likely meet some monsters. These monsters are learning tools so that the character can overcome and return victorious to their normal world, bringing their newly found courage, strength, and wisdom home to benefit their family and community. A list of some of our favorite monsters is provided on the following pages.

This chart is a suggestion of how to form a therapeutic campaign based on the Hero's Journey.

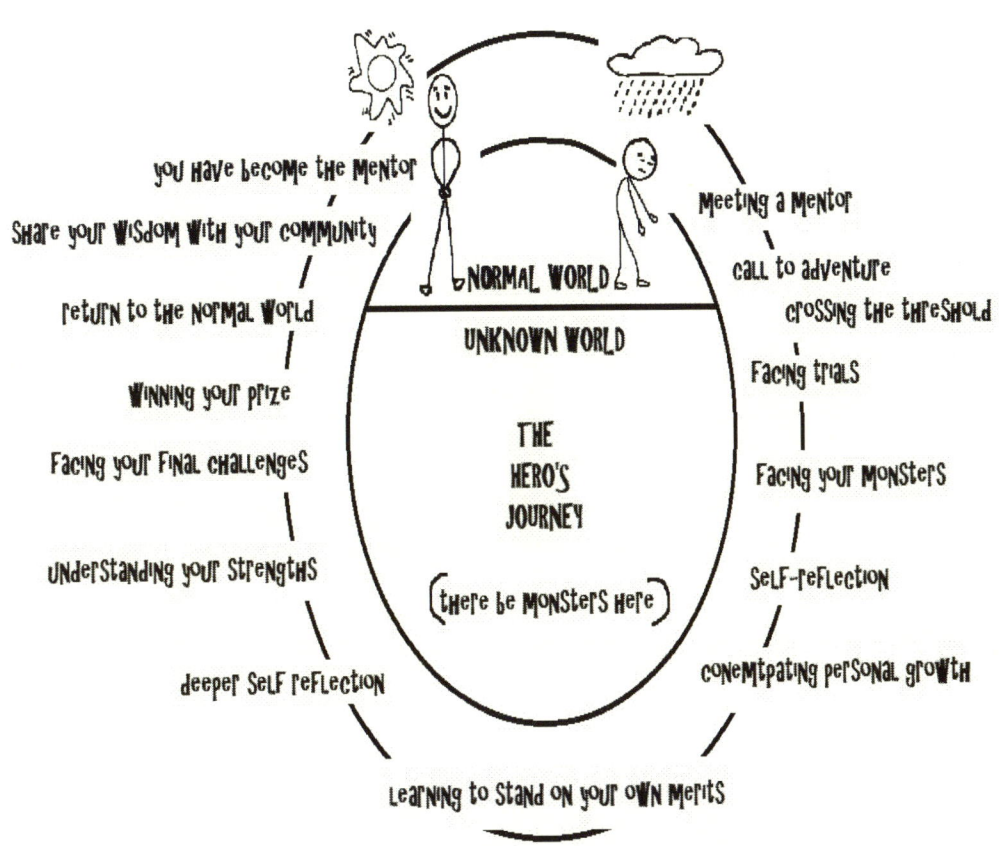

Useful Monsters

There are many monsters that the clients can meet, and overcoming a monster is always beneficial, but when possible it is good to personalize the monsters. Here is a list of classical monsters that we like to use (Note, these are not all Dungeons and Dragon approved characters. This is, after all, a therapy group - see the section of the book about stacking your deck for more ideas):

- **Calypso (from the Odyssey of Homer)**

    Calypso is a creature that represents false love. Calypso will dance with you and sing to you and whisper sweet words in your ear, but his/her love is false love and keeps you away from finding your true love. Calypso will change into any form that it thinks that you want, often mimicking the form of a lost love or a unmet desire. It can also be used when clients are lost in the fantasy world of celebrities or fictional characters. Using this monster in the therapy gaming session can help teenagers understand their choices in dating partners. This is a good time to explain what a healthy relationship looks like, and what an unhealthy relationship looks like.

- **Sistutl (a legendary Native American sea monster from the Pacific Northwest)**

    The Sistutl is a three headed sea-monster that guards the homes of underwater dwellers. When the Sistutl is met, its two heads look at each other and the third head looks at you, then you are frozen until you tell it your worth in the world, or you will drown. In the therapy setting, clients sometimes don't understand their own worth or have a hard time verbalizing it, so we allow other people to speak for them if necessary (we really don't recommend allowing a client's character to drown because they couldn't state their self worth!). This presents an excellent opportunity to talk about strengths, self-esteem, and the definition of "worth."

- **The Tarrasque (Dungeons & Dragons)**

The Tarrasque is one of the most powerful entities in the Dungeons & Dragons world, and entire campaigns can be designed around its attributes and legends. To clients, it can represent an unstoppable juggernaut, the daunting challenge at the end of games, or even a sleeping beast to be avoided. The high amount of challenge such a beast can bring is daunting, and it is recommended that direct combat be a secondary option to alternative (and creative!) routes. This is a good way to explain to your clients how to choose their battles wisely (both in the session and in real life).

- **Cyclops (from the Odyssey of Homer)**

Cyclops is a perfect monster to represent someone that only sees from one point of view, as represented through its single eye. The most efficient Cyclops that we have personally seen has been a Cyclops that was a good person at heart, but who held information (such as a map or a spell or other knowledge) that needed to be "cured" of its singular perspective. Once the Cyclops has been enlightened to be able to see other points of view, it is no longer a Cyclops in spirit, if not also in form. If necessary, it is possible to have a malevolent sorcerer place a spell on a client's character to show them the folly of their narrow point of view, but typically the clients will understand this concept by having a Cyclops to battle or to cure of a spell.

- **Doppelganger (Dungeons & Dragons, others)**

While the concept of an "evil opposite" did not begin with D&D, it does provide a framework to build a doppelganger of a client who may act against his own best interests or take actions against the group. This visible sabotage can be used as a metaphor for engaging clients on the topic of self-sabotage, or how actions can have consequences that may not be readily apparent. Doppelgangers can act as active saboteurs of the group's actions, or passive others with less-malicious intentions. The concept of what an identity is (and how it can be taken), or how an individual identity forms.

- **Sir-see (from the Odyssey of Homer)**

Sir-see is a monster that can represent pre-judging others. Sir-see traditionally feels that all males are greedy and up to no good, so she turns them into pigs without getting to know them. This is a good monster to help work through issues of race, gender, life-styles and more. Teenage clients may identify this sort of thinking as a person that they know in the real world, which can opens a rich dialogue between group members.

- **Sirens (from the Odyssey of Homer or Merfolk from D&D)**

Sirens are a type of merperson that lives in the water, usually guarding a magical coast from invaders (or adventurers). Sirens sing hypnotic songs of the past so that the listeners forget about the present or the future. If a character listens too much about the trouble from their past, (or glory days, more commonly in older clients), then they will not be able to appreciate the here and now, and it can be difficult to see a path to their future. For teenagers this can be helpful in getting over a crush that did not work out, or some feeling of injustice. This is good monster to use when there is a client that is stuck in the rumination cycle.

- **Oozes and Rust Monsters (Dungeons & Dragons)**

Oozes and Rust Monsters share a common trait: their ability to destroy the equipment of adventurers if given the opportunity. Having their hard-fought equipment damaged or lost can force clients to make due with what they have on hand, or open the door for discussions regarding material objects, finances, socioeconomic status, and how value is determined. We recommend generally allowing the characters to learn about the potential material damage that such a monster can do prior to the client encountering one. A noted observation from the authors is that such losses during the game session can bring up some difficult memories and challenges from the 'real world' (e.g. a clients unforeseen financial loss, material hardships, homelessness, etc.). These monsters also make good teachers where entitled clients are an issue and makes for a good conversation about "need vs want".

- **Hall of the Lotus Eaters (from the Odyssey of Homer)**

The Hall of the Lotus Eaters (aka The Pleasure Palace) is a place that is full of monsters who are known as The Lotus Eaters. These Lotus Eaters offers lotus flowers to adventures. Upon stumbling across the Hall of the Lotus Eaters, the client's character is greeted by several beautiful and friendly people that offer them lotus flowers to eat and drink. What is happening in this scenario is that the lotus has a mind altering effect on the characters and the characters lose track of time and their commitment. Anything more that just a few seconds in the Hall of the Lotus Eaters will result in days, months, or even years of life passing them by. If the character can realize what is happening and leave quickly, or if a character refuses the lotus, then he/she has a chance to explain the situation to the other characters and save the group. This is a good monster to use to open a dialog about drugs and alcohol. In the opinion of the writers, this is probably the most powerful 'after game' discussion that we have noticed. It is no surprise to most experienced therapists that children are more exposed and affected by drugs and alcohol than they typically will talk about in individual or family sessions. The Hall of the Lotus Eaters is a powerful tool in the book of a DM-therapist. Use it wisely.

- **Hydra (from the Odyssey of Homer or Dungeons and Dragons)**

Hydra (aka The Lernean Hydra) is a multi-headed dragon type monster that can be used to symbolize the need to get to the root of the problem and identifying our source emotions. The hydra can be fought by cutting the heads off of the monster one at a time, but each time the wrong head is cut off, the monster becomes angrier and more dangerous. Until the character gets to the root of the problem, the monster will continue to grow. A good use of the hydra is to explain anger. Anger is almost always a secondary emotion (not a standalone emotion). Anger has a reason that it has surfaced and generally has more than one reason (e.g., fear, envy, sadness). If you use the hydra in your therapeutic session, you might consider referencing Robert Plutchik's theory of eight basic emotions, or Book Two of Aristotle's "Rhetoric" or even Charles Darwin's "The expressions of the emotions in man and animals." References to these text can also be printed out and held back in case a conversation happens between the players or the characters. As an aside, one nice way to keep the session in the characters world, is to have some "down time" for them to talk and review their adventure so far. This down time might take place in the lobby of their lodgings or even a quiet spot in the town square, or on the bank of a river if they are camping. If necessary, an NPC may be introduced to start the conversation going about the emotions behind the Hydra, such as a food server in the town square or a fisherman on the banks of that river. The NPC can start the conversation off by saying that he/she has heard about their interaction with the Hydra and is curious about hearing more details.

- **The Suck (from a Cherokee legend)**

In Tennessee, there is a river that has a strong and dangerous whirlpool. The whirlpool is so strong that the old ones used to tie a large clay pot to a tree limb that stretched out over the whirlpool. The legend says that the whirlpool is actually a monster called "the Suck" that lives under the water in a home and all of the people that were not paying attention to the pot in the water drowned and were forced to live in it's underwater home. This is a good monster to in a for several reasons. One way is for paying attention to what is around you and for thinking about pitfalls that you might have in your life that you need to pre-think. In the therapy gaming session, therapists might consider having each player write down something that they would benefit from pre-thinking and ask their character to place the paper in the pot in the water in order to pass through the area of the whirlpool. If the Suck (the DM) reads the scroll and decides that the character has given the Suck the wisdom that it needed, then the player can pass without further trial, but if the Suck decides that the character has not passed the test, then the character has to go into the home of the Suck and the other characters must decide to rescue him before they can move on. The second way that this monster might be used is to decide which friends are sucking you down to into their lifestyle (despair, poverty, bad choices in life) and the scroll in the pot can be written about how or what the client/character might want to avoid).

Non-player characters (NPC's)

Non-player characters (NPC's) are characters that the DM-therapist has created to help move the adventure along in a particular direction. The DM-therapist (or therapists, if more are running a session together) will role play these characters. Sometimes these characters are developed to represent people in the client's lives that are significant, such as a parent, teacher, or sibling. Non-player characters can accompany the adventurers if the therapist feels that it would be helpful, or a non-player character may be isolated to a particular spot in the story (e.g. a librarian that never leaves the library, but is a good source of comfort as the client's characters come and go on adventures). Non-player characters are often a way for clients to experience of a deep and meaningful conversation with a person in their own life via role play.

For a non-player character, you may want to prepare a brief backstory (e.g., who are they and how did they come to be at the location they are in today – are there brothers or sisters – what mistakes have they made in the past – what do they want to happen in the future – what motivates them to think the way they do about certain topics). The richer the non-player characters are, the more thought the clients will be encouraged to put thought into their own characters. Clients with richer characters can pull these ideas from their own experiences or desires, making the therapeutic process stronger.

An example of when a non-player character was used during a therapy group was with a teenage client, whose parents reported a lack of respect for elders in his life, particularly his grandfather, who was a retired military veteran. His therapists introduced a very old dwarven innkeeper in a remote dwarven village. The inn was lined with paintings depicting scenes from various dwarven battles, and behind the bar was a dwarven broad axe - a symbol of war. The adventurers arrived at the inn and were given rooms. As they sat and waited for their adventure to begin, they took up conversation with the innkeeper and found that he was a mighty warrior. They listened to the dwarves in the inn tell about how he saved their lives and how he was a hero of the people. The teenager's parents reported that after this session, the teenager had a new interest in his grandfather and their relationship improved.

Maps, puzzles, contests, and other things that will make you think

In addition to social and combat interactions that take place in D&D, contests of wits and cognitive skill are also commonplace. By planning ahead using enticing information, you can divide up your information and store it in different locations and encourage players to ask questions about it and investigate it, even if it does not initially seem relevant to the adventure. This can give therapists an insight into a client's interests, which can be further written into the session. Take care that the puzzles or challenges that you present during the session are age-appropriate enough to be solved by the group, but not so simple that it appears that you are "giving" it to them without. Some of the favorite puzzles and contests that we have used in the past with clients include puzzles from talented and gifted student material for very adept client groups.

For example, simple riddles can be used as a puzzle. DM-therapists can have piece of paper ready, with a riddle such as, "Forward I am heavy, backwards I am not." The object is to work as a group to solve the puzzle to achieve a story goal, such as gaining entrance into a door that has a alphabetical keypad on it. When the client's characters work together to figure out the answer is "TON", they feel a sense of accomplishment and can move onto the next part of the game session. Clues can be given by non-player characters or by the DM-therapist if needed, but the object is to work through non-threatening stressful situations together.

Another puzzle that was presented to one group of teenagers that spoke various languages, was to write a series of notes, two in Japanese, two in Spanish, and one in Gaelic, and one from a favorite book of a client's. The notes lead the clients to secret passages within their base of operations. This helped each of the teenagers be the expert in the room and speak to the others and feel valuable to the group.

One puzzle that makes use of props used in clinical settings is the "Nail Stack" puzzle, used by researchers at Roger's Memorial Hospital to help clients overcome low self esteem and help solidify group unity. This puzzle involves the DM-therapist bringing in several nails and a board. Clients (characters) are told that in order to gain entrance into a castle, tomb, etc., that they must balance all nails on the head of a single nail. Sometimes frustration arises, which can be addressed by the DM therapist or a non-player character. Discussions about coping skills can be discussed during this time. Similarly, being unsuccessful at a puzzle presents an opportunity to teach skills about handling frustration, failure, and perseverance. They can also present an opportunity to teach appropriate responses to success and celebration!

At an end of one of the campaigns, the DM therapists gave a festival for the group finishing up a campaign (and the eight weeks of the sessions). The group members had requested a festival or party of some sort so they could practice social skills in a friendly setting.

The DM-therapists formed a medieval festival with flying pigs to catch and gnome pirates to kick (after being encouraged by the gnomes: they requested it! A difference to celebrate!). The youthful clients reported that having their characters enjoy a festival was very helpful to them because none of them had ever spent the day out "Just chilling with friends."

Stacking your therapeutic deck

The nature of D&D requires planning ahead by the DM-therapist, which can be highly beneficial, as it enables planning and designing interactions custom for clients. Group therapy for teenage clients is a dynamic and interactive process that is used for not only emotional healing, but emotional growth. Group therapy is also valuable because the close access to other teenagers in a controlled social setting allows clients to feel connected to other teenagers in a positive way (sometimes for the first time in their lives). The authors of this book believe that the best possible combination of clients for a therapeutic group would have a balanced combination youths and backgrounds, including maturity levels. It is also important to try to keep ages and cognitive abilities in mind when choosing group members, as groups can be overly frustrating and/or disadvantageous for clients.

Setting up your group dynamic is important. For our groups, we generally chose to limit groups to ages 10 and up. This does not mean that we are recommending that no therapist work with kids younger than this, we just haven't done it (yet!). Our focus has been on teenagers with social anxiety. The procedural and mathematical nature of character creation or D&D might require simplifying for younger players. With our youngest players, we have found that they like to "hack and slash" or just shoot out their magic for the first several sessions - testing their limits and bounds within the context of the universe. Four to six sessions into the therapy, these same youngest players start using their social skills to maneuver their characters (sometimes because they've run themselves out of spells or combat options, but often associated with a transition of interests). It is about this time that we notice a change in their confidence, both inside and outside the therapy group. Parents seem to typically report the same thing back to the therapists about this same time.

Part of "stacking your deck" is to keep in regular contact with the parents of the teens (assuming that the clients have not signed themselves up for therapy and want to keep their therapy separate from their parents, depending on age of consent and location). If a client is having trouble with a step-parent, it may be worth considering adding some sort of step-parent in to a campaign. If a client is having trouble getting their homework finished and turned in, then a campaign where the characters join a magic school and need to finish their spells may be guiding the clients in the right direction. Anything that a therapist would use in their day to day work with teenagers can be written into a D&D therapy group, making it fun for the client to begin to grasp what is being asked of them.

Group therapy for teenage clients is a dynamic and interactive process that is used for not only emotional healing, but emotional growth. Group therapy is also valuable because the close access to other teenagers allows clients to feel connected to other teenagers in a positive way (sometimes for the first time in their lives). The authors of this book believe that the best possible combination of clients for a therapeutic group would have a balanced combination of boys and girls and at least two of these teens that are socially mature. It is also important to try to keep age and cognitive abilities in mind when choosing group members. It can be overly frustrating and disadvantageous for clients to be put in with someone that is noticeably higher or lower in intellectual capabilities.

Setting up your group dynamic is important. For Ryan and Bev's groups, we limit our groups to ages 10 and up. This does not mean that we are recommending that no therapist work with clients younger than 10, we just haven't done it yet. With our youngest players, we have found that they can like to "hack and slash" or just shoot out their magic for the first several sessions. We have also noticed that about 4 to 6 sessions into the therapy, these same youngest players start using their limited social skills to maneuver their characters (sometimes because they've run themselves out of spells or the like). It is about this time that we notice a change in their confidence, both inside and outside the therapy group. Parents seem to typically report the same thing back to the therapists about this same time.

Part of "stacking your deck" is to keep in constant touch with the parents of the teens (assuming that the clients have not signed themselves up for therapy and want to keep their therapy separate from their parents, which is legal at age 14 in most states). If a client is having trouble getting their homework finished and turned in, then a campaign where the characters join a magic school and need to finish their spells may be guiding the clients in the right direction. Anything that a therapist would use in their day to day work with teenagers can be written into a D&D therapy group, making it fun for the client to begin to grasp what is being asked of them.

Going with the flow when clients do not

Sometimes new players (or challenging clients) will want to have their character leave the adventurer's party and set out on their own. There are a few tricks that DM-therapists have that can help get the group back together. An NPC can steal something from them. A character that has his/her favorite weapon or book stolen by a coyote, will most likely chase the coyote in the direction that you want them to go. A player that would like to collect money, may find coins on the ground in a particular direction. As a last resort, a magical creature can appear and take you to where the rest of the group is. Regardless, the end goal should be to reconnect the client with a group in a fashion that feels natural and without extensive railroading by the DM therapist. Before attempting these techniques, it is recommended to give the group members a chance to reintegrate and address the situation between them. Such an event provides a good teaching context for interpersonal skills.

Writing therapeutic storylines

When considering the type of campaign to run and story to tell, consideration of the specific diagnoses or difficulties that clients are working through is of high importance; for instance, a person with significant social anxiety may require a slower introduction into independent character actions and responsibilities when compared to a person working to develop better conversational skills. Below are several guidelines to consider with consideration to specific concerns:

- Highly stressful or combat-oriented events in D&D has the potential to result in an individual re-experiencing a traumatic event, so the responsibility lies with the DM to mediate the types of enemies and encounters, as well as set the tone for level of graphic content. Enemies like constructs, skeletons, illusions, and plant monsters inherently have less potential for gruesome combats as the characters battle them.
- Charisma-oriented situations (negotiations, social parties, audiences with royalty, etc.) present opportunities to focus on social skills and teach levels of appropriateness of various actions.
- Victims of abuse or neglect sometimes can present with feelings of powerlessness or indecision; in-game, the DM is presented with the opportunity for praising and rewarding active decision-making and appropriate assertiveness.
- Clients with difficulty focusing on tasks or impulsive behaviors may require more frequent redirection and reminding of the party's goals and current objectives. Smaller, contained events rather than long operations may benefit them more initially and build toward larger plots.

Building non-player characters

Non-player characters are characters that the DM-therapist has created to help move the adventure along in a particular direction. The DM-therapist(s) will role play these characters. Sometimes these characters can represent people in the client's lives that are significant, such as a parent, teacher, or sibling. Non-player characters can go along with the adventurers if the therapist feels that it would be helpful, or a non-player character may be isolated to a particular spot in the story (e.g. a librarian that never leaves the library, but is a good source of comfort as the clients' character comes and goes on adventures). Non-player characters are often a way for teenagers to experience sitting and having a therapeutic conversation with a person in their own life that is not currently possible otherwise, or even to practice such a conversation. The richer the non-player characters are, the more thought the clients will put into their own characters.

The magic is inside the client

Shared storytelling has a magical quality to it. A team of neuroscientists at Princeton University put a woman into an MRI scanner and asked her to tell a story. They recorded her telling the story on a computer and monitored her brain activity while she shared her story with them. Then they put a group of volunteers into MRI's, and had them listen to the woman's story through headphones while they observed their brain activity. As the volunteers listened, the researchers observed that their brains were synchronized. When the woman's frontal cortex lit up, so did the volunteers'. Simply telling a story, the woman was able to share the experience of her story with the volunteers that were listening. In other words, by simply telling a story, the woman was able to influence the emotions of the volunteers that were listening.

During a Dungeons & Dragons group session where clients are sharing stories, they are transferring their emotions to each other. Their brains are synchronizing, and they are sharing their desires, and their experiences with one another. When the group needs to solve a problem, or unite together against a common foe, their brains are working in unison, on the same set of emotions. Collaborative storytelling allows for each member in the group to share a set of beliefs and emotions with the other members of the group. For people with social anxiety, this is an experience that they may rarely (if ever) get outside the therapy session, and this is by no means a small experience.

Story plots, whether in 'real life' or in the context of a Dungeons & Dragons group therapy session, are made up of common events, linked by a common theme, and occur between selected characters that are controlled by the clients. As the story takes shape, it beckons the clients to share thoughts and feelings, in an "anything can go" type of atmosphere. There are very little rules to adhere to when you are part of a fantasy world, except those of social convention and communication. This premise, under the guide of a DM therapist, allows clients to add or hold back as much of themselves as they are comfortable with.

In typical (non-D&D) group therapy, clients sit and discuss common topics and themselves. This presents a challenging scenario for clients with social anxiety; even being asked to think about participating in a group with other people can result in an increase in symptoms of anxiety. In Dungeons & Dragons group therapy, the clients may be still anxious about being in a group of people dedicated to overcoming issues, they are also aware that the focus need not be on themselves personally, but on their chosen character, which is designed to absorb much of the client's anxiety. In a traditional group therapy, the focus is often on "problem-saturated stories", which can be anxiety provoking, or depressing, while during the Dungeons & Dragons group therapy sessions, the opposite presents itself: a focus is on "overcoming-problem stories".

The core purpose of creating stories is not so much to further a game, but to offer to write a story that the client will find valuable and healing. The story should be, at least on some level, an abstract version of what is happening in the client's own life. Clients naturally come to sessions with a pre-written story about their own lives and have the power to change that story at anytime. With curiosity and exploration, anyone's story can change. An effective DM-therapist is to remain in the background as much as possible, and let the clients co-discover their ability to heal themselves, through their artistic creation of an ongoing story.

Pro-social Coins

Pro-social coins are a way of promoting and teaching positive reinforcement within the group. At the beginning of each session, each individual is given 3 token coins that they can hand out to peers at any point. The clients are instructed to use these in situations where a person has been clever, helpful, or taken a positive action. These coins can be traded in in the future to the DM for skill points, ability score increases, feats, or a new spell (at varying exchange rates). The coins traded in must have been given to them by other players; the coins given by the DM must be given back if not handed out and are refreshed at the beginning of each session. A variety of items can be used as coins, such as spray-painted poker chips or metal washers.

Clients characters don't "die" in therapy

Obviously (or we hope that it's obvious), don't kill your client's characters off. If they get into a battle or if something goes terribly wrong, the characters bodies can be taken into the

Hourglass room for healing. If the group is far away and can not get the body back to the library in a reasonable amount of time, then the librarians can send a person (or several) to take the body to be healed. The character will be out of the game for a little while (or you can interact with the character in the Hourglass room while he/she is healing). If the group is still far away when the character is healed, DM action can be taken, such as using our librarians via the magic oak tree (aka librarian transport system) to deliver the character to (or near) the group.

On having a headquarters

The Library was developed by us to be a central base for campaigns. It serves as not only a place for the group to return to for rest and food and teaching about downtime, but also serves as a place of healing and reflection for the group. In addition, having a stable "home" for characters provides a place from which clients' characters, and by extension the clients themselves, can feel comfortable returning to, even after breaks from groups. A wide variety of rooms have been added over time to the library for the characters to explore and become familiar with.

The rooms in the library have been well thought out. Here are a few examples: the bathroom is a place that the players can go if they want to change their appearances (and their alignment, class, race, etc. if they are truly not happy with their earlier choices). The throne room on the second floor allows for the players to use bigger campaign items, such as an airship or a silver dragon, in the library. There are hidden rooms in the guise of broom closets, and there is an Ever-Changing Room that can be used as a DM sees fit, as forest, desert, or any other plane they desire. The players may encounter the librarians themselves, who can be useful as a DM tool for rescuing players that don't know what to do and are in danger, and of course for adding humor and mystery to the campaigns. The Hourglass Room can heal any character that is hurt or sick, transporting their bodies back in time while the Labyrinth is an ever-evolving hedge maze, and can be a campaign of its own if desired, similar to the Ever-Changing Room. The Mirror Room can be used as a portal to transport players to their "hearts desire" or serve as a literal place of reflection.

While all of these rooms work in the game for the characters, the therapeutic process for the players works in a similar fashion. By allowing the imagination to be free to experience these healing rooms, it is hoped that the client will also be free to experience the healing of their own minds. A client that is experiencing stress outside the game, might remember the path of the mirror, or the bed in the Hour Glass Room, and have a moment of peacefulness come to them. Alternatively, the bathroom can be used to allow clients to explore change in an anxiety-minimizing fashion, knowing they can return to a prior form as needed. The world created by the DM is a world that has no need for hours worth of video games, or arguing with their parents about cleaning up their rooms. This is a world where the player understands the value of using their intellect to study the topics at hand, keeping their gear organized, and walking through the forest instead of sitting in front of a computer game. For several of the players that the authors of this book have encountered, RPG's serve as a wonderful alternative for video game addictions.

Here is a schematic of our library (we are very proud).

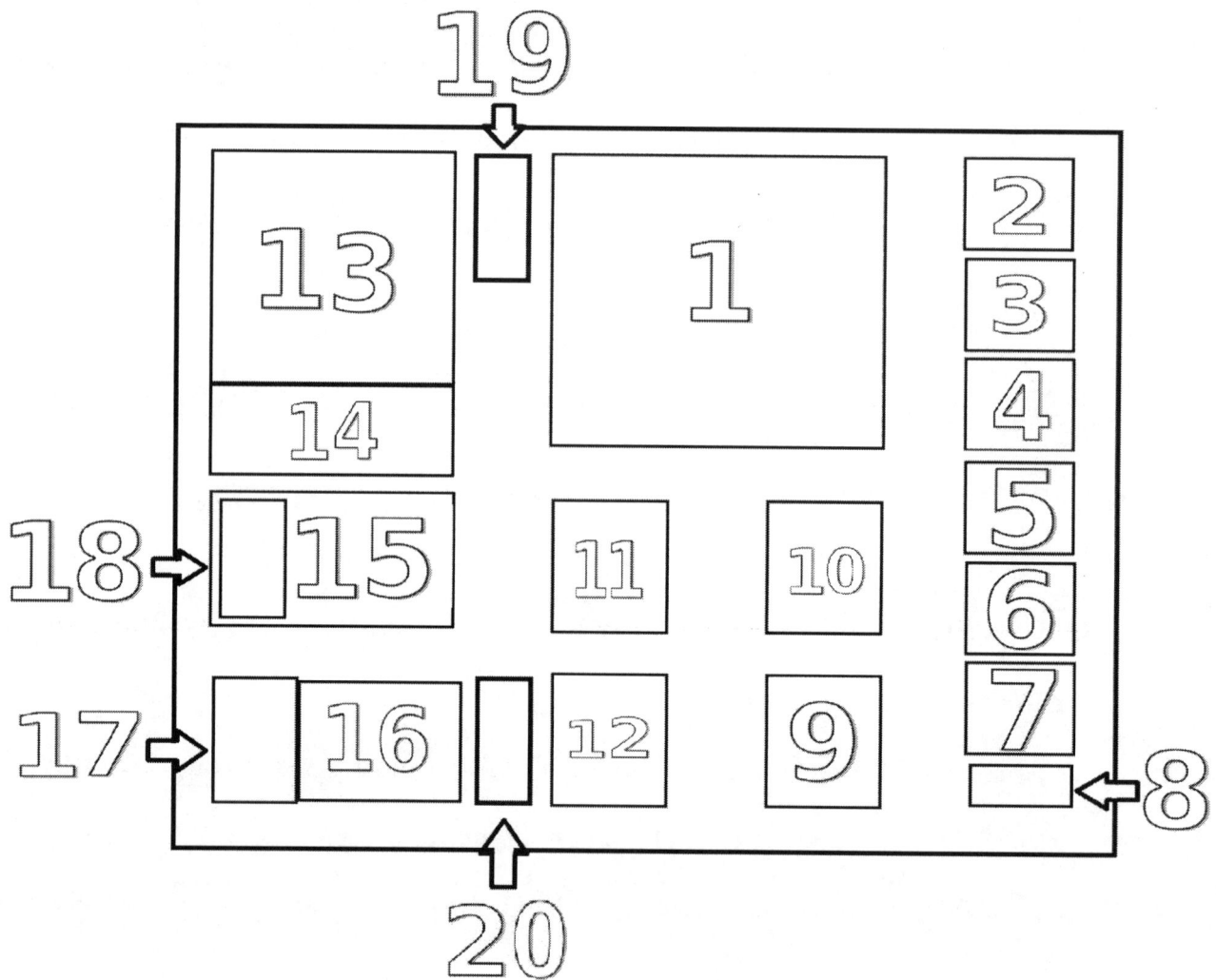

Room 1: The main room of the library. The oak tree will pop in here when it is needed.

Rooms 2 - 7: Guest bedroom. The front is for sleeping, the back is for projects.

Room 8: A storage closet. There may or may not be a hidden room inside this room.

Room 9: The room of lost things. Lost things can reappear in this room, but beware, they are flying around in the air and it takes some skill to get your things back if and when they appear.

Room 10: The Hourglass room. Contains a large hourglass that can heal characters, undoing their wounds as if they had never happened. In extreme circumstances, it can bring a character back from the dead. Pretty cool.

Room 11: The Ever-Changing room. Forest? Desert? Snow capped peak? It can all be found inside this room at one time or another, and so can all of the creatures that live there. Quite a space saving room if you think about it.

Room 12: The mirror room. Choose a mirror and step through it.

Room 13: The Ever-Changing labyrinth. Multi-levels. Interesting creatures. Lots of birds here.

Room 14: The magical garden. Need herbs and spices for dinner? Magic water from the fountain? Then this is the room for you!

Room 15: The kitchen. Every house needs one, but not every one is as well-stocked with fare for all races to enjoy..

Room 16: The bathroom. This bathroom features two magical bathtubs. Pop into one bathtub and change your whole persona…. But which one?

Room 17: The balcony overlooking the ocean.

Room 18: The personal room of the librarians.

Room 19: Stairs to the dungeon.

Room 20: Stairs to the attic.

On "problem" players:

Social conflicts are a common topic of mental health counseling, and also in D&D. One key difference, however, is that the context of the conflicts can be mediated through the group and the DM in the latter. How to handle such individuals? Natural consequences are often effective: if a person breaks a law, injures an innocent, or commits a similar wrong, consequences will reasonably follow (e.g., police involvement, vengeance-seeking relatives, etc.); moreover, the other players in the group will also be affected by such consequences, adding a social consequence! Another useful technique is to have the clients proactively confront the disruptive player about their behaviors using their characters. By using their characters' voices instead of their own, clients learn how to be mindful both of how another being would perceive a problem, depersonalize it from the offender, and are actively practicing problem-solving skills.

Understanding the basic rules of the game (the real ones)

This section has been placed in this book to help therapists that are new to role playing games and/or D&D to understand the basic rules of the game. This is a "super simplified" explanation of how to begin to play and is in no way meant to be the entire rules. For the full rules of the game, you will want to read and study the D&D manuals (or the rules of whichever role playing game that you choose to use in your sessions). The authors of this book have used D&D exclusively for their sessions, however there is no reason why another role playing adventure game would not work as well. One great thing about using D&D for your session is that a D&D group can be found pretty much anywhere in "the real world", which means that the client can find a social group once he/she has left the therapy group.

Clients will invariably come to the sessions with varying levels of experience with role-playing games and the DM therapist must take the role of game teacher. Games that ruled similarly to D&D, can take long periods of time to teach. One way to take some of the pressure off of "new" DM therapists, is to minimize the rules used (removing, adapting, and parsing rules for beginning players). This will help decrease confusion and improve the experience of the clients who are also new to the game.

When a DM therapist first in introduced to the game, the therapist may feel a bit overwhelmed at the amount of rules that exist. It may be a good idea to let the clients know that the game that they are playing may or may not be using "rock solid rules" during the session. This disclosure will help the DM therapist have leeway to make errors until the DM therapist can learn the rules. This should also help provide flexibility for clients new to the game.

Here are the three basic parts that will help you guide this game of chance:

1. The DM describes the environment to the group.
2. The DM asks the players what they want to do (they can all do separate things if they choose).
3. The DM describes the results of the players actions.

These three parts are somewhat influenced by die rolls.

So how does the DM keep the game a "game of chance"? There are seven dice (do not panic here - keep breathing). You will almost always just be using one die at a time, and which to use are explicitly given by the rulebooks. These seven dice are called, "d4", "d6", "d8", "d10", "d12", "d20" and "the percentile die" (or "second d10"). The "d" stands for dice and the number behind it stands for the number of sides that the dice has; when rolling multiple dice, the numbers of each respective type of dice is placed before the "d" (e.g., rolling 4d6 would consist of rolling 4 6-sided dice). The main dice that you will be using is d20 for most tasks.

Each weapon is assigned a damage die (e.g., a dagger is small and naturally will do less damage than a heavy crossbow).

- D20: This dice has a couple of unique features that can be integrated to sessions, namely "critical fails" and "critical hits." When a player rolls the 20 side up, commonly referred to as a "nat 20" or a "critical hit," whatever the character was attempting to do, usually happens in the game without fail. For example, if a character tries to jump a tall fence and get to the other side, the player would roll for it and it the d20 lands with the 20 side up, then the character is successful, regardless of skill or extenuating circumstances. However, if the d20 lands with the 1 side up, then the character has experienced an "epic fail". During epic fails, something negative happens to the attempt and it does not succeed. As DM-therapists, we try to make epic fails as funny but gentle as possible (remember the rule that no one permanently dies in therapy). Most major tasks, such as a test of skill or attacking an enemy, use a d20.
- D4: A d4 is usually used for smaller weapons. For example if you have a dagger the amount of damage that you are able to do with it when you hit a troll will

depend on the roll of the die. Rolling a 4 does the most damage possible for a dagger. Rolling a 1 does the least amount of damage possible for a dagger.

- D6: A d6 is used for medium sized weapons like a short bow or a great sword. As with all rolls of the die, the larger the roll the more power the weapon had at the time of the roll.
- D8: A d8 is used for larger weapons such as battle axes and war-hammers. As with any roll, the larger number, the larger the damage.
- D10's: A d10 is used for even larger weapons such as a heavy crossbow or a pike.
- D12: A d12 is one of the least-frequently used die, most often used to roll damage on heavy melee weapons such as a great axe.
- D100 (aka Percentile Dice): A d100 is used so that the DM can read their charts to decide random spells, effects, or treasure. The percentile dice that is used to determine items or effects from large charts. For a particularly explosive example, there is a character called a Wild Mage that casts spells and if they fail (if they roll a 1) then there is a special chart for them to determine which random spell was actually cast.

"I am finding out that people think I'm responsible. I've always felt responsible, like a person that others could count on to do the right thing and take care of things, but I didn't know that other people saw that."   Half-Elf Sorceress (age 15)

CHAPTER 4

Setting up the first session

Choosing a character class

Helping your client choose a character for the session will be a major early part of the therapy process, since your client will be role-playing this character for the next six to eight weeks. Many clients that are new to D&D will choose characters based on who they identify with at the tune of their first session. As a DM-therapist, you will want to be able to explain the characters a bit. There are eleven basic classes for Dungeons & Dragons characters that are available (the term 'basic' is used here, because there are other characters available, but these are the most common). For therapists that are not familiar with the Dungeons & Dragons vernacular, it might be easier to think of a "class" as a "job."

Opportunities/Challenges with each class

- Barbarian: The barbarian is loosely based on the iconic characters of Conan the Barbarian (written by Robert E. Howard) and Kothar (Gardner Fox) and to a lesser extent, Fafhrd (Fritz Lieber). The barbarian is an archetypal warrior who uses strength, rather than wit, to navigate the world. Barbarians are traditionally known to hail from areas where life was harsh and the strong ruled over the weak. Of all of the character classes, a particular challenge can present for the player in that Barbarians begin the game illiterate and have to expand extra resources to learn to read and write. Barbarians are able to fly into rages, which will make them stronger for a short while, then leave them exhausted.

Clients that are having trouble with impulsivity may choose Barbarians at first, which is a great opportunity for the DM therapist to guide the client into realizing that while there are some advantages to being the biggest and strongest in the group, there are even more advantages to learning to read and write and be thought of as wise. Clients that have had PTSD experiences may choose a Barbarian as their character to feel powerful and protected for a while.

- Bard: The Bard is loosely based on the iconic character "The Pied Piper of Hamelin"(a legend from the Middle Ages, stemming from the town of Hamelin in Lower Saxony, Germany). A Bard is a musician/entertainer that uses their artistic talents to create magical energies in the world. A bard is usually seen as a traveler that plays songs, tells stories, recites poetry, or otherwise entertains others. A bard uses his talent for entertaining combined with a variety of magical prowess to advance his group (e.g. playing an enchanted song on a lyre to stop a war). By nature, Bards tend to be unbound by laws or strict codes of conduct.

Clients that choose Bards often may be trying to relate to their artistic and creative selves, although clients that are not artistic will eventually attempt to roleplay a Bard as part of character experimentation. Bards also can appeal to clients seeking a sense of independence or variety. DM-therapists can help the Bard client express themselves by adding adventures where the Bard "sings from their heart" or otherwise taps into the artistic energies inside themselves.

- Cleric: Clerics are religious healers, empowered by their deity's blessing. Clerics are among the most powerful healers of the group and possess natural magic spells to cure themselves and their group members should they become injured. Clerics do possess magic spells other than healing, and can fight. Clerics are also able to repel or control undead creatures (depending on their alignment).

    Sometimes clients choose to roleplay a Cleric because the game party "needs" a Cleric to heal the party after a conflict, and other times a client will choose to play a Cleric because they feel that they have a healing or supportive nature. One challenge that the DM-therapist should be aware of is that clients who have some knowledge of the game, sometimes come to session believing that the group must have a Cleric. DM-therapists would be wise to make sure that their clients know that if they want to roleplay as a Cleric, it is great, but if they are choosing to roleplay a Cleric only to have one in the group, they are better off choosing a different character to play to avoid disheartening or demotivating them.

- Druid: Druids are loosely based on an archetypal form of educated naturalist class or people that studied nature in the area of Gaul, Britain, Ireland, and other parts of Europe during the Iron age. Druids are able to control some aspects of nature and cannot wear metal. Druids sometimes have an animal companion and have a unique ability to shapeshift into various animal forms. A druid is a powerful magic user and can learn spells from elders or years of experimentation, in formal or informal settings and tends to have an aspect of neutrality about them to reflect natural balance in the world.

  A client that chooses to roleplay a druid may be looking for a connection to history or the natural world. Some clients are drawn to the character of the druid because they long for a sense of spirituality and belonging, but need their own individual space. A DM-therapist might introduce some Celtic-Druidic philosophies into the sessions, since a focus of the druid belief system conveys the idea that people are meant to be a part of a community as well as a part of nature. To be part of a community, a family, and to learn to be on your own at the same time is also a main theme of existential therapy and a teenage reality.

- Fighter: Fighters are loosely based on soldier archetypes. A fighter is a generic class of warrior that fights using skill and strategy to achieve a goal. Fighters come from all walks of life and tend to have varied background stories.

    A client may choose to be a fighter for many reasons, including having been told that he/she has impulsivity issues, or has a need for physical interactions, however, many quiet people role-play as fighters to give them a chance to see what a different personality would be like for them. Fighters are amongst the most straightforward characters to build, making them friendly for new players.

- Monk: The character of a Monk is inspired by the fictional martial artist in the "Destroyer" series of books (Warren Murphy and Richard Sapri). Monks specialize in unarmed combat and typically emulate different styles of martial arts (e.g. jujitsu, aikido, tae-kwon-do, etc.). Some monks do use weapons. Monks are considered to be philosophical in nature and represent a wise fighting style, often complimenting their martial prowess with supernatural feats of body control.

Clients may choose to roleplay a Monk for various reasons, but from observation, it appears that clients may be attracted to Monks because of their philosophical nature or combination thereof with martial artistry. If the therapist feels that this is the case with a client in their group, this is a good opportunity to introduce mindfulness and other eastern healing thoughts into the sessions. This might be achieved by using a non-player character from a similar background that offers wisdom to the clients' character, or by producing scrolls or books of a similar nature.

- Paladin: The character of a Paladin is an archetypal form, based on the fictional Papal Guards or the myths of King Arthur, as well as the fictional character Holger Carlson from the novel, "Three Hearts and Three Lions". paladins are typical "Knights In Shining Armor" and represent valor, honesty, and higher morals. Paladin characters are expected to demonstrate and embody goodness at all times. By nature of their role, paladins are required to follow a code of conduct in keeping with their moral standing.

Clients that are drawn to roleplay a Paladin, may be wanting to experience a different way of life, or a character who projects goodness/righteousness. Clients that are drawn to the paladin may also be of a religious nature, as that is the source of a paladin's magical power.

- Ranger: The ranger is a character form based loosely on indigenous peoples across the world. Rangers are proficient as hunters, guides, trackers, or some other outdoorsy type activity, but their true calling is to defend the forest from the outside world. Rangers, similar to druids, can use spells to direct energies from nature, but to a much lesser degree. They are familiar with plants and animals, and often have an animal companion. Rangers are also known for their unique fighting styles, often using a bow or with a weapon in each hand.

  Clients that choose to roleplay a ranger may be expressing their connection to nature, or their lack of it. A DM-therapist may want to add components to therapy sessions that include Native American healing stories to the sessions for these clients. Rangers can be a very flexible class for clients to choose due to their ability to choose quarry and track.

- Rogue: The Rogue is an archetypical form based loosely on such iconic characters as Bilbo Baggins (J.R.R. Tolkien), Robin Hood and

Blackbeard. Rogues are spies and thieves, in the sweetest sense of the words. Rogues tend to be tricky characters that can get in and out of locked rooms and are quite capable of figuring out how to get past guards and dragons. Rogues sometimes have a secret goal, separate from the other group members. They are known for capitalizing on combat advantages or making sneak attacks.

Roleplaying as a rogue can present a large variety of opportunity for a client, including opportunities to make your own. Rogues don't have to follow rules, and they are often comic relief for others. A client that chooses to play a rogue may be looking for a way to relate to others in the group, or may be looking for a way to keep himself/herself separated from the others. A DM-therapist might try to point out social skills that the Rogue character has done that helps the others in the group, to help the client understand which social skills are solidly placed, and which social rules are bendable.

- Sorcerer: A Sorcerer is a person that has an innate magical ability (as opposed to a wizard, whose magic comes from studying). The word "sorcerer" comes from the Latin word "sortiarius", which means "one who influences, fate, or fortune." Sorcerers do not need to carry spell books with them. Rather, sorcerers are intuitive and can bring a larger number of spells to fruition, albeit with less variety. Sorcerers and wizards can think in opposite ways, such as sorcerers feeling that wizards are trying to imitate their natural ability by studying books.

Clients that choose sorcerers to role play might just be trying to have fun with their character, or might feel that they would like to have some ability to control the world around them. Playing a sorcerer presents a good opportunity for backstory in the form of how or where they obtained magical power: dark pacts, relatives as magical creatures, or even arcane experiments! Inexperienced or younger clients that choose a magic welder, like a sorcerer or a wizard, sometimes tend to use their magic spells up rapidly, which can be helpful to the DM-therapist, since after they have no magic spells left, the client is left to rely on his or her own creativity to get their character through the session.

- Wizard: The character of a Wizard is loosely based on the studied old man archetype, such as the iconic characters Merlin (from the stories of King Arthur) or Gandalf (from J.R.R. Tolkien's novel, The Hobbit). The word "wizard" comes from the Middle English word "wys," from which we get the word "wise." Wizards, unlike sorcerers, do not have an innate ability to cast magic spells, but rely on academic learning and practice if they are to use magic. Wizards must have access to spell books that are prepared in advance.

A client may choose to be a wizard because they are very versatile in-game or because a wizard is often an intellectual leader of the group. If a client chooses to roleplay a wizard, the DM-therapist might help guide the client into seeing that he is a capable leader. Wizards have access to a wide variety of arcane magic, but are more limited in the amount of times they can harness it per day. Some wizards choose to specialize in specific categories ("domains" or "schools") of magic.

Choosing character race

Race tells the player a bit more about the characters' background and the people in their lineage that preceded them. Race give us a basic physical description of the chosen character (for example, elves are more lithe than humans, while dwarves are shorter and stockier). These characteristics are important when judging if a character will be able to fit through a small crevice or be familiar with a particular language. This becomes important in therapy for teenagers when trying to sort out their own concepts and history about race, heritage, and family of origin. A DM-therapist can open a conversation about stereotypes pretty easily through the choosing of race, or the interactions that the characters have during the sessions game play, by using the race of the characters that are chosen or by using non-player characters.

Some questions that a DM-therapist might pose with youths could be, "What are stereotypes?" "What is race and does it exist? "What are racial stereotypes and how do you think they developed?" "Do racial stereotypes become self-fulfilling prophecies, or can they be changed?" "Are men and women in the same racial group viewed differently?" "What are the positive aspects about each character's race?" "Could a stereotype of a character change be depending on the characters' personal evolution?" For example, "How would a barbarian that studied to become a wizard be viewed by other barbarians, given that the barbarian culture prides themselves on things other than academic learning?" which can similarly translate to real-life topics, such as, "How would others in the client's worldview them if they graduated from college and became a lawyer or a physician's assistant?"

Below is a basic description of some of the most classic races based on Dungeons & Dragons. For a more detailed description, you will want to see the Dungeons & Dragons Player's Handbook or other guides for whichever respective edition you choose to use during your sessions.

- Dwarves: Dwarves are a thick, sturdy people that traditionally enjoy mining, fighting, and drinking. Dwarves stand about a foot shorter than most humans and tend to live in underground settings. Dwarves do not care for Orcs and have a hatred of giants. Dwarves often have a lawful alignment. Dwarves can see in the dark up to 60 feet.

- Elves: Elves are a physically thin people that live a very long time. Elves are introverts that value their privacy; they live in cities that are beautiful and filled with art or in natural settings where they strive to live in harmony with their natural surroundings. Elves have the ability to see twice as far as humans in low light conditions. Elves do not sleep and are immune to magic effects that may try to induce sleep. Elves sometimes make close bonds with humans, as evidenced by the number of half-elves.

- Gnomes: Gnomes are physically the smallest of the common races, standing around three feet tall. Gnomes pride themselves in being able to trace their lineage back to the ancient realm of the fey, where all true magic began. Gnomes are widely regarded as alien and strange by the other races because their culture is so secretive, and their hair tends to be the same vibrant colors found in flowers. Gnomes are prone to powerful fits of emotion, but find themselves at peace when they are surrounded by the natural world. Most gnomes have a strange fondness for unusual hats, headgear, or eccentric hairstyles. Gnomes have excellent vision in low light. Gnomes are overly fond of playing jokes, particularly on taller races, although their choice of jokes sometimes is seen as misplaced by other races.

- Halflings: Halflings are taller than gnomes, but shorter than dwarves. Halflings are brave and curious and excited to experience the world. Halflings are known for their optimistic sense of humor. Sometimes a halfling's curiosity will override their good sense, which lands them in trouble. Halflings are often charismatic "people persons" and often strike up conversations with others along the path randomly. Halflings prefer to walk barefoot because they have very tough bottoms of their feet, and in the winter they grow a thick covering of fur, making their own naturally warm boots. Halfling like to have a nice house to base from, and often leave their house in order to have adventures that they can tell to others around their fireplaces in the evening. Halflings are loyal friends and family members.

- Half-Elves: Half-elves are the offspring between a human and an elf. Half-elves are sometimes viewed by elves as a sad combination, because their lives will naturally be shorter than a true elf, but yet they are come from an elven family and are welcomed as an elf. Humans, on the other hand, can view half-elves as a marvelous combination, partly because half-elves will live considerably longer than other humans, and they have a natural ability to use magic, which humans' do not have. Half-elves are a dichotomous lot: many spend a lot of time alone or in insular communities while others become highly social (sometimes with mixed results).

- Half-Orc: Half-orcs are a strange and rare combination of human and orc and are generally feared and distrusted, sharing the reputation of their orc counterparts. Half-orcs stand between 6 and 7 foot tall and have large canine teeth that grow out of their jaws. Many half-orcs have grown up with only one parent, because orcs and humans consider the other an inappropriate fit and rarely interact with each other. Most half-orcs have grown up in difficult situations that only another half-orc could truly understand. While orcs can appear somewhat dim-witted but strong, half-orcs can be very resourceful, but are considerably weaker than an orc (but stronger than a human). Both are known for their cunning more than their academic pursuits. These misunderstood creatures tend to be are met with suspicion wherever-ever they go.

- Humans: Humans are a common species and can feel that they are the dominant race in the world, based on their populace alone. Humans run the gamut from being savages to nobles (and everything in between), possibly because human society comprises of a multitude of governments and lifestyles. Because of their sheer numbers, it is not possible to give a strong description of a human, except that they are probably the most diverse race that exists at this time. Most humans are given to wearing clothing, possibly because like elves, most of them lack any protective hair or fur. Humans are a highly flexible race for clients to play and offer the familiarity of being their true race outside of the game.

Choosing character alignment

Alignment is a category of moral and ethical perspectives that clients will choose for their characters. Non-player characters and other creatures also have alignments. There are three types of alignments, "lawful", "neutral", and "chaotic" and three types of axis, "good", "neutral" and "evil." Players choose where their characters fall on these two scales to describe their core personality tendencies.

- Lawful alignment characters are characters that follow the law that is set for them. These characters are convinced that order and laws are absolutely necessary to assure proper order prevails. Alternatively, they may have a strict moral or personal code they hold (or are held) to.

- Neutral alignment characters are characters that tend to decide for themselves whether rules are something they want to follow. Most neutral characters will follow the law for sake of convenience or in day-to-day life, but will not follow if it goes against their own personal beliefs or becomes too inconvenient. Alternatively, neutral alignment characters may understand the reasons and logic behind laws, but decide that they should not apply to them (for whatever reason).

- Chaotic alignment characters are characters that can be impulsive and make decisions based primarily on whim. They may enforce anarchy and actively work against formal systems or simply be apathetic to what the laws may be.

- Good axis characters are characters that are empathetic and try to "do the right thing" for others. They can be charitable towards friend and foe, acting for the better interests of all. For example, a good axis character would not be willing to make a deal with a corrupt government, no matter the amount of gold that he was offered.

- Neutral axis characters are characters that can take either good or evil actions, depending on what is needed. For example, a neutral axis character may decide to make a deal with a corrupt government if he were offered a lucrative deal or if it helped their family. Neutral characters may also be actively working as antagonists to both good- and evil-aligned characters simultaneously.

- Evil axis characters are characters that choose to do things that are against their party or others, acting in personal interest without regard for the impact their actions will have and often fail to empathize with others. Evil characters may try to conquer or enslave others, or focus on building personal power.

The following table will give the nine possible combinations for character alignment.

Lawful Good	Neutral Good	Chaotic Good
Lawful Neutral	True Neutral	Chaotic Neutral
Lawful Evil	Neutral Evil	Chaotic Evil

Talking about character alignment can also be a very opportune time to have an important conversation with your client about their own morals and judgements. This is a great opportunity for the therapist to talk to the client about which attributes are important to the client and if necessary, how to separate the roleplay from the client's actual beliefs. This does not mean that the therapist should discourage a client from choosing an alignment for his character that is not similar to their own alignment. Roleplaying, after all, takes a bit of acting ability and while being able to identify with the character that the client has chosen will make that acting gig easier, some clients will want to attempt to role play other people in their lives, or attempt to roleplay a character that seems interesting to them that they would never have been able to experience any other way, except during a roleplaying game. As a DM-therapist, it will be beneficial to try to help the client sort out which alignments are a part of the client's thought processes and which belong exclusively to the character.

During the first session, sometimes new clients will choose an evil alignment. This can of course be for many diverse reasons, (e.g. having frustration that needs to be addressed, trying to understand or mimic a sibling, feeling that an evil character will gain more attention, etc.). There is some therapeutic value for clients that choose to roleplay an evil character, since during the roleplay of an evil character, clients are allowed to express their aggression and even engage in behaviors that would be considered inappropriate (or impossible) outside of the game session. It will also allow them to be faced with the results and challenges that negative choices may bring. This type of fantasy permission can be a psychological relief from those aggressive feelings. Once some of the feeling of aggression has been lifted from the client, the situation that created the hard feelings becomes easier for the client to handle. As a therapist, which character alignment the client chooses should allow a path for a deeper understanding of what is going on in the client's real world.

Filling out character sheets

Character sheets are needed to keep track of your character. Character sheets can be found in Dungeons & Dragons books or online. Character sheets can be daunting to clients who are not familiar with them. At times, we have cut down the character sheets into a more basic format to minimize distraction from the session and enable clients to learn the system more easily. This can be useful for players new to the gaming experience by bringing a focus to the most important aspects. Over time, the DM can introduce other features and sections.

The purpose of a character sheet is to figure out (and keep track of) the character's numerical qualities, such as health or experience points. Categories for character sheets include character strength, dexterity, constitution, intelligence, wisdom, and charisma. Also on the character sheet are details such as what kind of equipment (weapons, food, armor, etc.) your character has with them, how many hit points he/she has available, any feats or skills the character possesses, etc.

A few pre-session rules (they're more like guidelines, really)

- Rule #1: The DM has the final say

The DM-therapists in the room are, first and foremost, therapists. We don't like to be the authoritarians in the room (in fact, we really hate it). Ideally, clients find ways to work out their own issues and we believe that the group should be allowed this opportunity; however, if there is a conflict or a difference of opinion and it appears that it cannot be solved by any other means, we reserve the right to have the last and final say in the matter.

- Rule #2: See rule #1
- Rule #3: What happens in D&D, stays in D&D (mostly)

While the tool being used for therapy is D&D, it is important for clients to remember that this is a group therapy session, which means that anything that another group member says should be treated as confidential and not be shared outside the therapy session. Characters, however, are not group members, and groups can choose to develop rules about what is or is not acceptable to discuss in this context. Group privacy is important to discuss during a first group with clients. Similarly, conflicts may arise within group and should be addressed with the group members in person. Previous clients have called this rule, "Nothing about me, without me." Should a client be absent from a session, we recommend a simple story-related reason for their character to be gone, such as, "Remained behind resting" or "Is in town running a personal errand."

- Rule #4: No touching other group members without permission (yes, that means you).
- Rule #5: Be respectful to one another - we want this to be an amazing journey for everyone.
- Rule #6: No touching other group members belongings without permission (which includes dice, miniatures, and character sheets).
- Rule #7: Please feel free to suggest new rules!

For any other rules that members want to add, we recommend that they be unanimously agreed upon by the group AND approved by the DM.

Supplies that you will need

Please keep in mind that if you plan on starting a Dungeons & Dragons therapy group, you will want to have access to three core books: the "Dungeon Master's Guide," the "Player's Handbook," and the "Monster Manual." You will also need a set of dice for each DM therapist and each group member. Dungeons & Dragons uses a variety of dice with more sides than "regular" six-sided dice. A set of D&D dice generally contains one 4-sided die, one 6-sided die, one 8-sided die, two 10-sided dice, one 12-sided die, and one 20-sided die. These are often referred to as "dX" with X representing the number of sides on the given die. You will also need copies of the character sheets to keep score on, and a pencil (recommended instead of a pen because you will need to be able to erase). You will also need a large table and chairs for your players. Conference rooms, classrooms, or group study rooms can all be excellent locations for a session.

Understanding the basic rules of the game

From a conceptual point of view, Dungeons & Dragons is a pretty simple game with a thorough supporting rule set; from a focused point of view, though, it can be perceived as the opposite. The basic idea is for the player is to decide how their character will act and within the world the DM has set for them. From the DM's administrative point of view, Dungeons & Dragons can be a bit more complicated, so here are some basics of the game to offer a bit of help to therapists that would like to become DM-therapists. This chapter in no way is going to give you all the rules for Dungeons & Dragons - you're gonna need to get yourself a rule book.

You will need to choose an edition of Dungeons & Dragons and editions themselves have varying degrees of rules. This is best done before the group is announced so that clients will not have to spend time discussing about which version they want to use. The **authors of this book are proud to announce that they use with a streamlined version of Dungeons & Dragons 3.5** (we changed some of the rules to fit our needs) or 5th edition, however, any version that you care to use will be fine, as long as you work consistently within to it. The authors of this book decided that 3.5 worked the best for therapy sessions, based on its ease of use, historic accessibility, and its freedom of choices. 3.5 can be a complicated edition to learn, in part due to the vast reference material produced over time, and as such, a more streamlined recent variant (such as 5th) may be beneficial to those unfamiliar to D&D.

After or during character creation, start out your world by describing where the adventurers are in a "you" context, not a "we" context, since the DM is expected to be the narrator. The better the description that you give of the world and its content, the better the visual that the clients will have to work from. For example, "You are in a large field with cattle in it" could have been expanded to, "You are lying down, and have opened your eyes and have found yourself very sleepy, having woken up in a large field with tall yellow and red weeds woven throughout the green grass. Around you there are some sort of long haired, but strangely domestic cattle. The smell of the grass seems pleasant, but as you gain your strength, you notice the smell of fresh cow manure becomes stronger…." The clients will have questions (probably every few seconds), so be prepared to be creative and paint the best picture that you can. A note about descriptions: when describing a person or character (other than basic non-participating entities, like cows), describing the physical attributes of the character works best, because that leaves the emotional feelings to the client to work out (e.g. "Beside the fireplace, an older woman sits, knitting with a silvery thread" instead of "A gentle, kind woman sits beside the fireplace, knitting with a silvery thread"). This avoids giving the players knowledge that their characters would not have otherwise: in this example, they would have no way of knowing if a woman is gentle or kind if they had never met.

Maybe the hardest thing to learn as a DM (or a DM-therapist) are when to roll the dice. You will be rolling dice for any creature that you have put into your adventure, and you will also be telling the player's characters when to roll their dice. One thing to keep in mind that might help, is that you will be rolling the 20 sided die (aka d-20), unless indicated otherwise. Dice are mostly used for deciding how a character does when his player wants to attempt a task (such as a lining up for a battle, or climbing a hill, or trying to sing a song to win over a pirate).

Typhon the Dragon, son of Gaia and Tartarus, mate of Echidna. Woodcut circa 1530

"I think part of my problem is that no one ever talked to me when I was in public school. I'm not sure it was because of the medical issues, or if they just didn't like me, but I know that no one ever talked to me. No one ever invited me to be a part of a group before the D&D group here. You have no idea how much that group means to me." Half-Elf Cleric (age 14)

Chapter 5

The first game session and beyond

The first session

The first session tends to be the most formally structured and in which the DM-therapist will takes a more frontal role. They will lay out rules for the group, make introductions as appropriate, and gather expectations and goals for the players. The first sessions is generally used well to create characters and collaborate on the type of world in which the adventure will run. Another key feature is establishing how the players' characters will have known each other or previously interacted, if at all.

Typically, the beginning of the day's adventuring begins with a review of the last session, the goals/objectives of the party, and any complicating or time-sensitive factors. As with group therapy, D&D groups often take place on a weekly basis, and a review can be helpful in reminding the group of where things were left off. Reviewing the last session also offers an opportunity to process any conflicts that may have emerged and give feedback.

Handling the unexpected

"No plan of battle survives contact with the enemy" is a maxim that holds true in D&D. Much of the power of D&D comes from its flexibility and the ability to make worlds custom-suited for player tastes and needs; however, this power comes with a price. A world that is very open allows participants to have a large degree of freedom. As such, players may engage in antisocial behaviors (e.g., stealing, aggression) or refusal to participate in various situations. This presents the quandary to the DM of getting "stuck" in freedom - shall the players be allowed to maintain the freedom of the world if they are engaging negatively? Below is an example of a storyline to begin and list of common "sticky" situations a DM may encounter, as well as suggestions for handling them.

Example of a storyline

"You have been having dreams of a forest that is near the ocean. In the dream, you are standing on a dirt trail that is strewn with cedar boughs. All around you, you can see huge dark green Boston ferns that come up to about your waist. The trees are cedar, and they give out a fresh and exciting smell of a fresh earth and brings to mind damp soil and living things on and underneath the forest floor. The world is alive and it appears to have just finished raining. The salty ocean breeze pushes this scent gently past your nose and you turn your head so that you can take in more of the smells when you notice that there are hundreds of rhododendron bushes that are just starting to show their pink buds. It occurs to you that you are standing in an ancient forest that probably dates back to the near beginning of time. The sound of a seagull can be heard on the ocean side. The seagull seems to be far away and although seagulls are known for living in flocks, this one somehow seems alone in the world.

Further down the trail you notice there are other people. A woman dressed in leather armor looks around from a high spot on the trail. She is quiet. She is wearing a gray hood that covers most of her face. A man with two swords on his back stands even further down the road. He notices you, but he quickly listens behind him. He appears to be waiting for something. Two identical twins of no particular gender step out of the shadows of a particularly large tree and seem to be quietly whispering to each other in a different language. They make eye contact with you. You awake from this dream, and the urge to find this place in the forest overcomes you. Beside your bed, you find a map wrapped with a cedar rope. The map was not there the night before. What do you do?"

As the DM-therapist, you will of course have already designed the storyline before your first session. The more detail that you can add to the description and the feeling of the place, the richer the experience of the adventure will be, and your clients will be more engaged. If you are not good at making up places for your story lines to take place, then one idea for you is to use a place that you have been before and spin it in a different light. The magical forest told in so much detail in the example above, is a place that one of the authors grew up in (she is describing the Siuslaw National Forest on the Oregon Coast).

A village that the adventurers might come across (or even start from) might sound like, "The streets were narrow and made of a gray cobblestone. Some of the stones were missing and in need of repair. To the left side of the street the shops were sparse and appeared to be mostly temporary huts that were selling produce. A large burley woman was arguing with a short thin man about the price of blue eggs. The argument seemed to be interesting because people were gathering behind them to listen attentively. As you approach, you can make out comments in the argument about whether his blue eggs held more magical power than her green eggs.

On the other side of the road was a bread store. Inside the bread store there were four people working. The first adult male was taking bread out of the store window, while the second adult male was checking the large stone oven to see if the bread was ready. The two smaller people appeared to be children who were mixing something in a large bowl.

Beside the bread store was a patio where some musicians were setting up the band stand for the day. One of the musicians looked familiar. You remember seeing his face on a poster in the jail. She was a fugitive, but you cannot remember why."

These types of details when starting your story, will give the clients many choices to make decisions from. Do they work together and why? What do they investigate and why? If you are a clever DM-therapist, this might be a good time to try to understand and guide their thinking process. Having (or learning to) think ahead is a valuable tool for our clients to be able to understand and use.

Group conflicts

Interpersonal interaction is the format of all groups and, as people interact and challenges approach, conflicts within the group are a real possibility. We have found it beneficial to allow the group to naturally engage with each other to work towards resolving conflicts, mediating as possible in a similar fashion as to group therapy. Similarly, negative antisocial behaviors a character may make in-game (e.g., stealing from NPC's) presents a novel opportunity for the group to engage in therapeutic discussions around such behaviors, as well as previously-referenced natural consequences. D&D also allows for DM-based consequences from NPC's, from as mundane as an upset neighbor to as extreme as an offended deity. We do recommend trying to resolve conflicts as expeditiously as possible to prevent conflicts from persisting between sessions.

Timing your ending (watching the clock)

Timing and planning sessions can be one of the trickiest factors of using D&D as a therapeutic tool, both logistically and therapeutically. Ideally, a session will reach a predetermined ending point as part of the ongoing storyline. A good ending point is represented by a point in the story where characters are in a stable state and not in immediate danger, such as directly after wrapping up a major encounter or before embarking on a new leg of the journey.

While a therapist is often familiar with watching a clock to time sessions appropriately, a DM-therapist may benefit from a clear representation of time for clients, such as an hourglass or alarm, that will remind players 15-30 minutes before the sessions ends so that they have the opportunity to wrap up the activities or actions they wanted to take prior to the end of the session. If there is time, a brief wrap-up of happenings and reiterating of therapeutic skills being built is also beneficial.

The Arabhar Dragon (aka the Arab Flying Snake) woodcut, circa 1450

"They tell me that my son has social anxiety. All he did before was sit at home and play video games. It was a battle to get him off of that computer, we couldn't even get him to go to school. He didn't talk to other kids except for the ones that he knew over the computer. We couldn't even get him out of bed to go to therapy before, but now, he looks forward to going to therapy every week, and he gets on me if he thinks we are going to be late. I can see the improvement for sure. I'd wondered how playing a game could possibly be therapy, but it's working. I'm closer to getting my son back. He started a Dungeons & Dragons group with his cousin now, and he sees other people outside of therapy. It's so good to see him talk to real life people. Whatever it is that is happening, it's working." Father of a Half-Elf Fighter

CHAPTER 6

Thoughts about interventions by diagnosis

About diagnoses in general

In the world where therapists are held ever-increasingly accountable for quantifying gains and justifying services to managed care organizations and insurance companies, the concept of a therapeutic group using a role-playing game might appear difficult to accept at first glance. As such, several forms have been included at the end of this book which can be used as pre- and post-group measures to quantifiably demonstrate outcomes (mood improvement, etc.). The success of this group has been also anecdotally measured by both group members, parents, as well as the clients' individual therapists. This next session will attempt to give therapists some ideas for storylines based on diagnosis. It is important to remember that sessions story lines are best written when the character that is played is dealing with a situation that is similar to what is happening in the clients' personal life.

Social Phobia/Anxiety and social skills

Probably the number one diagnosis we have referred for clients entering into a Dungeons & Dragons therapy group will be social anxiety. No matter which storyline a therapist writes for clients with social anxiety, some benefit is likely, since Dungeons & Dragons is, by design, encouraging clients to participate in face-to-face interactions and on-the-spot conversations. A therapist might consider writing a non-player character into the session that has a more extreme case of social anxiety that clients, which can help the clients by allowing them to help the non-player character with coping skills. If the social anxiety is particularly high, it is also possible that a client might even consider making his or her own social anxiety a quirk of their character, at least for the first session, or until the client is more relaxed. Story lines that have downtime can be written into the sessions, such as time spent waiting at headquarters, getting to know each other. Sibling sets can be helpful if the siblings get along somewhat, since they will have a familiar face in the group. Story lines that have been suggested for clients by parents include times when the characters are having meals together, choose to investigate a new town, or meet the families of other characters. Story lines that have been suggested by clients themselves include fairs, concerts, and having meals in their own homes.

In a mainstream culture, it can be very difficult for people to find interactive experiences, once they are past the early childhood/school phase of life. Playing with friends becomes bound by "acceptable social activities" such as going to a bar, or a concert, a sports event, or a house party. For people that have social anxiety, these venues can be scary and are often met with avoidance, whereas role playing games are one of the few activities where participants can be social, and also explore their imagination and express themselves through a common shared story, which makes it a wonderfully healing experience for people who are feeling isolated and anxious. The difference between a role-playing game like Dungeons & Dragons, and other games, such as board games such as Monopoly or card game such as Uno, is that during role-playing games, the player must put something of themselves into the game. Wherein Monopoly a person is focused on getting all the possessions, and in Uno a person is focused on getting (and getting rid of) the best hand of cards, in a game of Dungeons & Dragons the player must use social skills and logic to further himself and others through the game. This sharing of self with others that is the true healing part of the experience.

When our clients were younger children, they learned about the world by playing games, fantasy games included. These games gave our clients the ability to understand themselves in the context of the world, and the chance to understand others. By the time that our clients are teenagers, many have forgotten how to play. This lack of play stifles creativity and imagination, which make interactions with others, difficult, and anxiety provoking. Play is a vital part of social interactions, both in youth, and in adulthood. A suggestion to DM-therapists, would be to be open to getting carried away with a little bit of play, and your clients will follow.

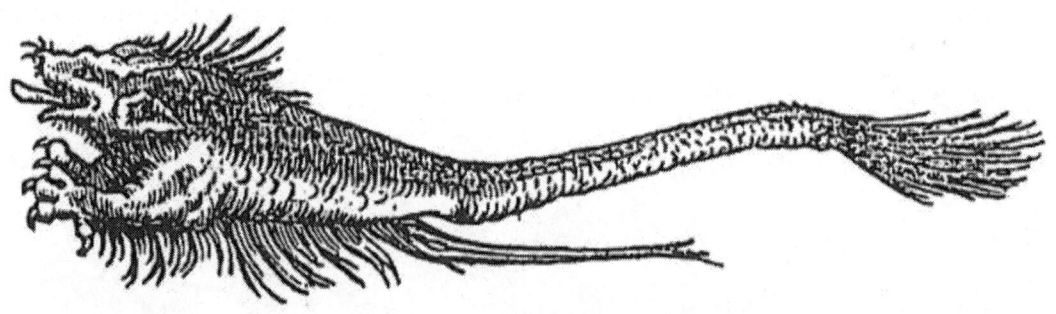

Rosmarus Morss Piscis Dragon, drawing by Juan Eusebio Nieremberg, 1910

"People like me, we can be complicated. You just can't grow up the way that I did and just open up and start telling people about your life. That would scare most people away anyway. With doing this, playing a part like this through my character, I can let people get to know me first, get to know who I really am. Then, when they get to know the real me, then I can open up and talk." ~ Human Rogue age 15

PTSD and Trauma

Trauma can present a unique challenge to address due to factors associated with D&D - namely, combat. If a client has experienced violent or aggressive traumas, an in-game combat situation may run the risk of triggering an episode of re-experiencing the trauma that the client is not prepared for. To handle this, a DM-therapist has several options: they may choose to avoid physical combat, pre-clear it with a specific client, or to engage in combat with non-living or - threatening entities (such as a golem made of clay or a being made of light). Knowing a client's history is important in making such decisions. Alternate challenges, such as puzzles or tests of skill and physical prowess could be used in place of combat. Clients should be encouraged to speak up or feel free to sit out, should an uncomfortable situation present itself. Trauma-informed care is a key component of therapy and using this methodology should be no different.

The idea for therapeutic game play for trauma is not new. In 2004, American military doctors and researchers found that by using a virtual reality game called Virtual Iraq, the client could successfully work through familiar traumatic experiences in the safety of the hospital. This game play exposure lead to an increase of the client's ability to recognize, cope with, and control their responses to the traumatic situations. Of the clients in the research, fifty percent experienced significantly fewer flashbacks than they had previously encountered. Similarly, using an RPG to address past negative events in a client's life in a safe setting to teach coping skills can benefit clients.

Adjustment Disorders

Adjustment disorder is a group of symptoms, such as anxiety, stress, or sadness that occur while a client is going through (or has gone through) a stressful life event. These symptoms occur when the client is having a hard time adjusting to the new situation and generally present for a more limited amount of time, focused around and after this stressor. Adjustment disorders are quite common, diagnosed in 5-20% of clients seeking out care It is recommended that clinicians pay attention to symptoms of Adjustment Disorders over time to maintain diagnostic certainty: the diagnostic criteria are specific around time limits and context of stressor, and Adjustment Disorders may be simply presenting as a placeholder for other mental illness. Symptoms of Adjustment Disorder can mimic depression, anxiety, or conduct/behavioral-related disorders.

Adjustment Disorder treatment appears to work great during Dungeons & Dragons group therapy sessions, because the client (or the DM-therapist) is able to write sessions that address the presenting issues at hand, whether directly or indirectly. For example, a client that is having a hard time adjusting to a parent's divorce has virtually unlimited options in the Dungeons & Dragons realm to explore their feelings (e.g., Their character might come from a home where both parents are still together, or their character might have a sibling that is in love with an half-orc, or their character might venture into a land where all children are born from beakers and are shared by many parents, etc.).

One thing about adjustment disorder is that it is so common that other group members have most likely experienced an adjustment disorder of their own. Breaks can be taken from the game session to address stressors in the client's life, without breaking the flow of the game session. One of the beautiful things about Dungeons & Dragons therapy is that it often turns into an "impromptu talk therapy session." Building skills to cope with stressors and transitions in-game can benefit clients Adjustment Disorders.

Depression, Dysthymia, and mood disorders

Depression and dysthymic disorders are mood disorders that result in a persistent feeling of sadness and loss of interest, often coupled with trouble with energy and sleep. If a client is experiencing a severe depressive disorder, then a game session may not be as helpful as if the peak of the depressive symptoms have been alleviated. However, for clients that feel that having some human interaction in a safe and comforting environment might be helpful for them, then this type of group session may work for them. Depression and its "younger sibling," dysthymia, can affect how a client feels, thinks, and behaves, and can lead to a variety of serious emotional and even physical issues. Once a client and their therapist feels that it is appropriate to attempt a group therapy session, the group therapist and the individual therapist and the client might consider meeting to discuss what can happen during the group sessions. If all three are in agreement that a Dungeons & Dragons therapy group is worth trying, then the group therapist will want to watch for things like a loss or gain of appetite, loss or gain of emotional responses and expressions, and game play that involves feelings of hopelessness or joy, as well as typical interactions with other clients. It is suggested that only one client with depression be allowed into the group, because of the group tendencies to follow the energies of one another. Research and experience tells us as therapists that when a person with depression is put into a group with people that do not have depression, the outcome for that person will be higher than if that person is put into a group of others with depression. The basic rule here is the same as before: always stack your deck (and the deck of your client). You want to provide the best healing that you can provide.

Clients that have described that the worst symptom of their depression is the feeling that they are isolated and have lost their connection with others, are excellent candidates for group therapy. For these clients, the best treatment is sometimes, interacting with others during a relaxing socializing and safe manner, in order to regain that feeling of connection. Role playing games certainly provide a feeling of connection with others and are also widely available outside of therapy sessions.

"I have autism. That's a spell that can't be broken. But I can use other spells to counteract it, like smiling and making eye contact. Those are pretty powerful spells, and they count as double if you use them on humans…. Of course it all depends on your roll, but in real life you get to roll again and again and again and again." ~ Elf Wizard, age 17

Autism Spectrum Disorders

Autism Spectrum Disorder is a neurodevelopmental disorder that impairs a person's ability to communicate and interact with others. Autism includes Asperger's syndrome, which is believed to be part of the Autism Spectrum. The term Asperger's syndrome is currently not included in the diagnostic manuals, but it is included in this book because some clients tend to favor the term or have had this diagnosed previously, making it the most accessible language for them. Clients that have Autism and Asperger's can have very specific and limited interests or specific/unwritten rules to follow.

Clients with significant impairment in social, academic, and occupational functioning, may or may not be good candidates for group therapy. If an individual therapist believes that their client may benefit from a group therapy, such as Dungeons & Dragons, then they might want to have a conversation with the group therapist. Since Autism (and Asperger's) are spectrum disorders, each client can have different symptoms and needs. If it is determined that the client would benefit from being part of a group therapy session, it is then important to ask the client if they are interested in being part of the group. When clients that are on the spectrum tend to have very specific likes and dislikes, and also tend to have limited interests, they typically has some sort of social anxiety built in, and as a result, may reject a group at first. The authors of this book have found that with this type of client, it is sometimes wise to ask them if they would consider being part of a group, then give them plenty of time to get used to the idea of being part of a group, long before the group actually begins. Once the client agrees to think about being part of the group, we typically tell the client that they are on a waiting list, which gives the client time to get used to the idea of something new happening in their lives. This seems to be the best method yet, and also works for clients that are high on the social anxiety list.

During group therapy, a person with Autism has the chance to experiment with social interactions by learning as their character and following the leads of others. Pro-social coins are especially helpful (more on this later). Autistic youth may need a different type of guidance from their DM-therapist, but the experience is usually a rewarding one. A missed social cue can present as distressing or result in a reaction that requires guidance.

One piece of wisdom when working with youth with Autism is to give them plenty of time to be themselves and to experience their feelings in a way that makes sense to them. One example, is an Autistic teenager that the authors worked with, started out needing time to "hide" in his hoodie (often in the back of the room). Instead of addressing the "mood-swing" (as he called it), he was asked once if things were okay, and if he did not respond back, that was his signal to the rest of the group that something had upset him, and he needed less input. After the first eight sessions, he no longer felt that he needed to "hide". As a therapist, it is in our training to talk about everything that comes into the room, but sometimes it is good to set the training aside, and just let the client have a moment.

Attention Deficit/Hyperactivity Disorder

Attention Deficit Hyperactivity Disorder (ADHD) - or, commonly referred to as Attention Deficit Disorder (ADD) by some - are neurodevelopmental disorders that are characterized by problems paying attention, controlling excessive activity, impulsiveness, and/or difficulty controlling behavior that is not considered age appropriate. In teenagers, they typically have difficulty socially and academically. Despite these impairments, many teenagers have an exceptional attention span (called hyperfocus) for tasks that they find interesting or tasks that provide immediate reinforcement.

When accepting clients for group sessions, it is important to remember that when more than one client shares a diagnosis, the symptoms of that diagnosis will almost certainly have an impact on the rest of the group members (with the exception of social anxiety, which appears to improve when clients become more socially involved). These are no exception to this rule. One client with ADHD or ADD will typically try to follow the rest of the group and can respond well to redirection and prosocial input from the rest of the group members. Two or more ADHD-diagnosed clients can mean that they wander off task more often and will have more difficulty sustaining focus. From experience, it is suggested that a small number of youths with ADHD can work well for a group, but several individuals with attention and focus challenges present an increasing challenge. Once that teenager learns to overcome his hyperactivity, then another can be added with caution.

Impulsivity is a large part of ADHD, and that impulsivity combined with a lack of focus can mean that a client needs to be brought back to the session often. Also, a client with ADHD may mean that they may be socially intrusive and interrupt the sessions excessively. ADHD teenagers can appear socially immature, which may be frustrating to other players.

Talented and gifted and ADHD

A word about Talented and Gifted Children and ADHD and ADD diagnosis: One of the most common misdiagnoses could very well be of children who are gifted that are misdiagnosed as having ADHD. The gifted child's characteristics of intensity, impatience, and a need to know things fast can easily be mistaken for hyperactivity. As a therapist, please consider the situation and the setting where the symptoms arise. A truly hyperactive child will exhibit symptoms in all settings (e.g. at school, in scouts, at home, in the community). In the classroom, a gifted child's perceived inability to stay on task is likely to be noticed, even if the child is bored with the work due to a mismatched learning style. Children that are gifted may spend half of their time in their regular classroom, waiting for other children to catch up to them, which takes a ton of patience on their part and often results in the gifted child "acting out" (out of extreme boredom). The word hyperactive, is therefore a word that is used to describe gifted children, as well as children with true ADHD. It has been a pleasure, through the D&D process, to identify teenagers that have been diagnosed with ADHD, that are gifted. This is done by adding quizzes and other knowledge based or academic type stimulation to the campaign sessions. While the child who is hyperactive has a very brief attention span in virtually every situation, children who are gifted can concentrate comfortably for hours during cerebral activities such as Dungeons & Dragons without requiring redirection back to the task.

Electronic Addiction

For decades now, there have been debates in the mental health world about whether or not a diagnosis of "Electronic Addiction" should be added to the Diagnostic and Statistical Manual of Mental Disorders (DSM). As of the date of this book, no diagnosis has been added to the DSM-5 (the latest version of the diagnostic manual) and this probable diagnosis still remains an area of active research. The World Health Organization (WHO) is preparing to include it its new global medical coding guidelines. It is for this reason that the authors have decided to address this briefly.

In our experience with hundreds of youth, as with many behaviors there are a some youth who spend way too much time with electronics and, when the electronics are removed/limited, the youth appears to be in an emotional crisis, similar in concept to what happens when a chemical is removed from a person with a chemical addiction. Parents and caregivers are sometimes at their wits end to try and move their young person from the couch or to relieve them from their crisis mode, as such a crisis impacts both the youth and their caregivers/family. A good starting point to determine if a behavior is negative is to ask, "Is my engaging in this behavior impacting my life in a negative fashion?"

In using D&D therapy sessions, we have found that the typical youth will engage with others due to the "game format," seeing the D&D storyline is somewhat similar to a video game storyline. This presents an opportunity to practice face-to-face interventions in a more friendly and familiar setting.

"I'm learning that I'm a bit of a show off and I don't think people like that sometimes, but I'm still figuring it out." Drow Ranger (age 13)

CHAPTER 7

Wisdom Points Earned (case studies and practical examples)

Because of privacy issues, and our dedication to keeping our clients confidentiality as secure as possible, the authors have been careful to not include any identifying information in our case studies. Sometimes gender or age has been changed to protect the identity of the client. These case studies were chosen to help other therapists understand the power of the unusual group that is being presented here.

The Case of the Red Dragon (overcoming trauma)

Two the teenage siblings with a history of abuse wrote a backstory together. The story that they agreed on was about a red dragon that destroyed their happy home and their village along with it, and how the two half-elf characters managed to escape the dragon's fiery anger, only to witness their mother and their younger sister running for their lives in another direction. The story was detailed and had obviously been well thought out in advance. After speaking to the clients after the session, the clients revealed that their stories, were symbolic of their former abuse (the red dragon being the symbolic representation of their abuser). The DM-therapists arranged for the client and her sibling, along with the other group members, to defeat the red dragon. The teenagers and their mothers reported that this was a topic in their household for the entire summer, and it opened the conversation of the subject up so that the mothers and the children could talk together about what was formerly a forbidden topic.

Orville Redenbacher (cheating yourself)

Orville Redenbacher was a non-player character that was introduced when one of the participants was caught cheating (repeatedly). The DM-therapists made Orville Redenbacher into a character that was always getting caught cheating and arranged it so that the group offered to watch over him. Orville spent so much time cheating, that the client had no chance to cheat himself. Once it was established that the group wanted to get rid of Orville, a conversation about why Orville would want to cheat ensued. This appeared to help the client, who did not cheat after that. We have used Orville Redenbacher many times in various sessions. As a side note, not one of our youthful clients recognized the name, but the parents seemed to get a kick out of it.

The Drow (changing your world)

One of our teenagers came to the group, feeling that he was a "bad seed", due to PTSD-related difficulties. This teenager chose to be of the drow race (a dark elf, usually associated with chaotic-evil). This drow's backstory was that he was born to drow parents, and that his mother had been killed by his drow father, leaving the boy with the abusive father. The boy had been put into a drow military school, where he learned to fight, but that was not what he wanted in life, so he set out to change his life by embarking on an adventure with better classes of people. This story, the boy reported later, was an abstract story of his life. The DM-therapists were able to create opportunities for this client's character, where the character could be educated by a wizard, thus relieving him from his life as a drow soldier.

The Fighter (labels other people give to us)

One very shy teenager wrote a backstory about being a halfling fighter. Even though her character was only three feet tall, she was assigned the role of a fighter by her teachers. It was curious during this campaign, that this halfling fighter would never really fight (would run from pretty much anything, typically climbing a tree or hiding behind a rock). After several sessions, the teenager told the group that she had written the character to be like herself. Her teacher had put the title of "fighter" on her, even though she had only been in one fight in her life, and that fight came about because she was standing up to a bully.

Dwarven beverages (teenagers and alcohol/substance use)

More than once, a client has brought up the topic of alcohol during a game session. Since our clients are teenagers and are becoming more and more aware of chemicals like alcohol, the DM-therapists needed a way to address "finding beverages" in the story. It was decided to introduce "Dwarven Beverages" (you're not going to find that in a D&D manual, we made it up because we felt we needed it). If a character "found" a Dwarven Beverage (assumedly an alcoholic beverage), they had to roll a d20. If the client rolled between 1-3 the character would have no effects from the beverage. If the character rolled between a 4-7, the character would be sick to his stomach enough to lose a turn or the next five minutes of play. If the character rolled between an 8-11, the character would temporarily misplace something he owned. If the character rolled between 12 - 15, the character would not be able to stand up or walk. If the character rolled above a 15, the character would fall asleep (which means that if the group left, they would either have to leave him behind, or carry him with them). While our intent was not to frighten children away from alcohol, but to turn the discussion to the context - that the beverages were harder for non-dwarves to handle and could have negative impacts if not properly prepared or informed. We only had one client keep trying to push the beverage issue for one session, and after that he decided that his character was better off without it. That one day, his character had fallen asleep, and the group decided that they had to carry him with them, but to teach him a lesson, they decided to draw on him with a sharpie. They drew doodles on his face, and added the words, "Smart people don't drink and roll."

The airship pirate (domestic violence and its effect on children)

One of the most powerful sessions that we have had the honor of hosting, we often refer to as "The Airship Pirate". The story was that the adventures had been sent an airship with two small children on it (the group was to help the children sort out some family conflicts that had led to a split between the families). The characters and the children were in transit on the deck of the airship, when the airship was suddenly boarded by a pirate. Two of the older teenagers, stopped the fight long enough to give instructions to have the younger children taken below deck so that they couldn't see the fighting. What came next was a stop in the game, and almost an hours' worth of conversation about the effects of domestic violence on children. Four out of the six teenagers talked about their own experiences with domestic violence and the impact it had on their lives, while the other two asked questions and learned. After about an hour, the game play resumed.

The Sisiutl (knowing your worth)

One of the most powerful sessions that we have seen, involved a pair of real-life siblings, who were also siblings during their Dungeons & Dragons group session. The siblings had a severe history of abuse and trauma, and had managed to escape the abuse a couple of years before they became part of our group. Because of the trauma that they had experienced, these siblings both suffered from a feeling of low self-worth. During a campaign, the group needed to cross an ice-covered lake, and they were told that could see a large shape swimming below the ice. When the Sisiutl surfaced, it caught the travelers with its stare and froze them. The group was allowed to roll to see if they were hypnotized by the creature or if they had avoided eye contact with it and could move on.

One of the siblings rolled high enough that she was able to move away from the creature safely, and one of the siblings rolled low enough that she was hypnotized by the creature's stare and could not move.

The sibling that was hypnotized was told that she needed to tell the creature her worth in the world (why she is valuable, what is her worth in the world, what are her successes, what were her strengths). This sibling could not come up with anything and her character was about to drown and need to go back to the library to heal in the Hourglass Room, which means that she would have missed a day of the adventure (which is about ten minutes in real time). Her sister, whom she had been fighting with for about two months, asked if she could speak in her sisters place and the DM granted her request.

Her sister told her sibling that she was valuable because she had been there beside her through 'real' battles at their home, and had saved her life when she was suicidal, and had saved the life of their mother. The sister that spoke spared no details about how important her sister was to her and her family. The group (including the two therapists there) were teary eyed. The group took a break and discussed the importance of knowing your worth and how sometimes that is hard. There literally was not a dry eye in the house. The two siblings still talk about that day on the ice lake, even years later.

"For me, the group helps me experience different lifestyles and different points of view that I may not have experienced any other way, and it allows that in a safe and fun manner. That is therapeutic right there." Gnome Rouge (age 16)

"The thing that took me a while to figure out is, I am the DM of my own life story, and I can give myself as many temporary charisma points as I want to." ~ Human Wizard (age 21)

"My mom always told me not to hit, then I got bullied at school for about two years and she finally told me to stand up for myself, so I did, then I wound up in detention, but I'm not a bad kid. I chose my character to be like me. She's little, and she's labeled as a fighter, but she only will fight if she absolutely has to. She will stick up for the people that she cares about though. She is pretty much like me. I wish I was more like her." ~ Halfling Fighter (age 14)

Chapter 8

Worksheets and handouts

These are printable worksheets and handouts that you can use for your pre-sessions or post-sessions.

Welcome to the Library can be given out after the group has finished their first campaign. We prefer to roll the printed text up and tie it with a ribbon of some sort (just for a cool factor). This explains how the library works and adds some humor to what could have been "a chore to read". Clients do not have to read this of course, but the clients that do, will be more informed during the next group. It seems to encourage kids to read too… so here you go….. Enjoy!

Illustration by George Wharton Edwards of the Child Ballad, 1910

WELCOME TO THE LIBRARY

WELCOME TO THE LIBRARY

This text has been partially written and partially proofread by

the Librarians.

The magical library has its origins in the original Lost Library of Alexandria. It's a long story... google it. We don't have time to explain that to you now. Don't google it now though because you're supposed to be reading this scroll. What are you doing? Is that a phone in your hand? Put it away. Geez. Pick up a book. No, don't pick up a book right now…. It's a phrase…. Oh just keep reading. Pretty please? Okay, cool. Here we go.

LIBRARIANS

The library is run by a very intelligent group of small gray creature known as Svirfenbin (pronounced Svir-Fen-Ben - aka "Deep Gnomes"). The Svir-Fen-Ben prefer to not let others know they are in charge (we just don't like the spotlight much). These particular Svirfenbin prefer to be addressed as "Librarians", due to their dedication to the Magical Library.

Since these Svirfenbin Librarians are Deep Gnomes, they speak many languages including Common, Undercommon, Gnome, Dwarven, Elven, Giant, Goblin, Orc, Draconic, Terran, and a simple language that enables them to communicate on a very basic level with forest animals. Yep, they are totally smart. I mean, they have lived for thousands of years in a magical library.... Smart is a given.

Svirfenbin typically live about 250 years, but due to the magical properties of the library (in particular its Hourglass Room), the Librarians are significantly older than their natural lives.

The Librarians gain their knowledge of the outside world from others that have visited the library, or forest animals that bring them information in exchange for food. The Librarians are dedicated to helping others, and many times have allowed a group of people to use the library as a home base. Because of the use as a base for good, the Librarians and the library books keep a protective magic spell over the library that so far has successfully kept creatures with malicious intent outside of the library. Per one of the eldest of us Librarians, "This is also where we get meat. We mean a cougar or a grizzly or a wolf or something will occasionally bring us a deer or a rabbit for a stew. Rabbits and deer don't bring us cougars or grizzlies. That would just be ridiculous. There isn't any point in going there. Anyway, we don't kill. It's not that we're against it, we are Gnomes, we just don't have a place to put deer and elk and all of that. Ever try to keep a herd of cows in a library? I guess we do have the garden area.....Yeah, we do have birds in the garden, but they are for eggs. Do not eat our birds. They're pets. Pets that lay eggs. Egg pets. Whatever. Just don't eat the birds. That's a big no-no. We don't have time to explain all of that.... stars! We would be here all day! Okay, where were we? Oh yeah....us. Okay. Since we Librarians are exceptionally old Deep Gnomes, we have developed some magical powers of our own, most notably their ability to send dreams to others, and to transport a single person back to the library in times of danger (although using either of these talents causes great stress to the Librarian that uses it, so we prefer not to use it unless there is a life in danger). We draw straws and see who gets the short straw, and the loser has to go get you. If you make us do this, we will probably get even with you somehow. We're smart like that. We're gnomes for Pete's sake, not EMT's."

ACCESS TO THE LIBRARY

The main entrance to the library is through an oak tree construct that was developed for the library. A small portal in the library is available to take a person through to a single destination, but it does not provide a safe return point. Other portals may be available in the form of gold or silver doors… or mirrors… okay, so there are probably a few different ways to get in and out of the library if you really want to… you can figure it out on your own time. Return points through doors are random not therefore guaranteed. Other portals may appear and disappear. Gnomes can't control everything…and who would want to anyway… you know how much time that would take? Be reasonable.

BOOKS AND SCROLLS

Books and scrolls in the library are sometimes magical and sometimes ancient. Well, I guess they are all ancient. We just mean that sometimes they are magical and sometimes they aren't. Oh, never mind, you'll figure it out. The library has the ability to transform a person into a book if it is voted upon and approved by the Librarians. Many books in the library are writers that have been immortalized in paper to live out their eternity as their book. Most of them even asked to do that! Some.... well....they messed with the birds. I told you, we love those birds. We named the peacocks after our favorite beverages.

Books and scrolls can be checked out of the library by select people, but they are limited to one book or scroll per person at a time. If you have a book or scroll checked out of the library, you must return that book or scroll before you can remove a second book or scroll from the library.

It should be noted that some books are more willing to be checked out than others.

ROOMS AND FEATURES

Individual sleeping chambers are provided for adventurers. These sleeping chambers will only open to the person that it has been assigned to. Behind each sleeping chamber is a personal workroom space for each individual adventurer. Each morning, the Librarians will provide a breakfast for the adventurers in their rooms. All other meals will be provided in the kitchen area.

It is not suggested that adventurers drink any unmarked liquids in or from the library, since at least one of the librarians appears to be experimenting with magical dwarven beverages. Didn't know there was such a thing? Yeah, you come to the library, you'll learn stuff!

KITCHEN

The kitchen is open 24-7 for anyone that would like to prepare their own food or drink. If you are having trouble finding the appliances, try turning a bookshelf around. We like space-saving features.

BATHING ROOM

There is one bathroom in the library. The bathroom contains one toilet and two bathing tubs. All of your bathroom needs will be provided by the Librarians. It's like a spa in there! You ask, it will appear. As long as it's bathroom-related of course. We're not going to provide you with a pony or anything like that. Just shampoos and stuff. You can come out looking like a completely different person if you want. My cousin once went in a gnome and came out a bugbear! That was pretty cool!

HOURGLASS ROOM

This room contains a large hour glass that is able to heal even grievous wounds. It has been suggested that the room heals by turning back time, literally undoing wounds., but we think that is a myth (although we are still researching it – although we are definitely a whole lot older than we are supposed to be...so....yeah).

THE ROOM OF LOST THINGS

This room can replace items that have been owned by the adventurer in the past. It will also make you dizzy and forgetful. It is not advised to stay more than a minute or two in this room.

MAIN ENTRY ROOM

A large lobby designed to greet visitors. Yep, that's it...What? Did you think it was some magical room? Okay, there might be something about that room, but maybe not. Maybe so, maybe not. Sometimes stuff shows up on the table or the walls. Who knows for sure? Anyway, moving on...

MIRROR ROOM

This room contains a mirror that shows the true form of anything in the library. This room may also contain a small portal that can be used to travel to one destination.

LIBRARIANS' SLEEPING CHAMBERS

This is our place to chill. It's none of your business what goes on in there anyway. Keep on moving. Nothing to see here.

THRONE ROOM

Why do we call it a Throne Room? Is there a throne in there? No…..but I'm glad that you asked. This room is called "The Throne Room" because once upon a time it contained a large throne (it was on loan from some very amenable cloud giants), however it has also contained many other large items in the past. We probably should have called it the "Really, really big room", but "The Throne Room" just sounded so totally awesome, that it remains "The Throne Room." This room can fit large items. It is not clear how these large items come and go from this room, but rest assured that they do.

EVER-CHANGING ROOM

This room changes randomly. It has appeared in the past as a bathroom, an attic room, a basement, and a couple of times it has been a forest. The room tends to be unstable and random. Probably should have called this room "The Random Room", but that name was already taken.

DUNGEON (AKA BASEMENT)

This room is a dungeon (hence the name "dungeon" - I mean really.... how hard was it to figure that out?). There is something odd about this room because the magic that protects things from coming into the library, doesn't always seem to do much in the dungeon. This room changes depending on what or whom is in the dungeon. I'd just avoid going down there without a good reason. We recently found a necromancer setting up traps down there. We really need an exterminator, but where do you find a magical exterminator that will do dungeons? Maybe we need to try to get that thing sealed up better. Can we write that on the "To-Do-List," please?

GARDEN LABYRINTH

This feature of the library is very old and may have existed before the library was built. This garden contains a hedge labyrinth. The garden available to travelers and is a great source of fresh foods. There are probably something that you shouldn't eat. Some herbs and plants are great for magical spells. You just can't go around putting things in your mouth if you don't know what they are. There are also beautiful birds there. The birds are for eggs. Don't try to eat our birds. Remember, we can turn you into a book. A vegetarian cookbook. The labyrinth in the garden is home to many magical creatures. They basically open the labyrinth doors up when they want company, or they need something.

OTHER ROOMS AND FEATURES

Sometimes the library will add rooms or features. We don't know exactly why, we're not voting on it or anything (okay, sometimes we do vote on it, but not always). We can't really explain rooms that we don't know about, now can we? And if we did…..well, where's the fun in that? Go with the flow!

Bardic Poetry

These poem exercise's can be used to help a client conceptualize their character's backstory. If the therapist decides to introduce one of these poetic exercises to their group, please note that this is also good time for the therapist to suggest that the client's fill the poem out for themselves so they can see their own backstory.

Poetry is a wonderful way to get client's to connect more with themselves. If a client would like to fill the form out and create a poem about another person in their lives, this may help them think more in depth about that person (e.g. a missing parent, a difficult sibling). This form is of course optional, but the richness and understanding that comes from seeing your own story in writing can be a very powerful tool in the life of the client.

If possible, making copies of these completed forms and giving the client copies may help the client continue to think about the things that are in their own background that build up who they are. It has been the experience of the author's that client's that are interested in filling out a poetic form will sometimes "rework" the form for several months, trying to get the form "just right."

Therapists that find their clients have a tendency to ruminate on negative aspects of their lives, may want to challenge their clients to add more positive aspects of their lives to their poems, to create a more supportive backstory.

Two examples of each poetic exercise have been included here so that therapists and clients can see how they work. It is important to note that this is art, so it has no solid rules. Each client should be encouraged to change the format as much as they like, while keeping in mind the purpose is to tap into their feelings (or the feelings of their chosen character).

The first poem is inspired by the poem "Where I Am From" by George Ella Lyons. The second poem is inspired by the poem "I Am" by John Clare.

I AM FROM

I am from _____ (specific ordinary item), from _____ (product name) and _____ .

I am from the _____ (home description... adjective, adjective, sensory detail).

I am from the _____ (plant, natural item), the _____ (plant, natural detail)

I am from _____ (family tradition) and _____ (family trait), from _____ (name of family member) and _____ (another family name) and _____ (family name).

I am from the _____ (description of family tendency) and _____ (another one).

From _____ (something you were told as a child) and _____ (another).
I am from (representation of religion, or lack of it). Further description.

I'm from _____ (place of birth and family ancestry), _____ (two food items representing your family).

From the _____ (specific family story about a specific person and detail), the _____ (another detail, and the _____ (another detail about another family member).

I am from _____ (location of family pictures, mementos, archives and several more lines indicating their worth).

I AM

I am _____ (two traits that you like about yourself)

I wonder _____ (something that you wonder about)

I hear _____ (an imaginary sound)

I want _____ (a desire that you have that is not an object)

I am _____ (repeat the first line of this poem)

_____

I pretend _____ (something that you actually pretend to do)

I feel _____ (a feeling that is imagined)

I touch _____ (something that you touch in your imagination)

I worry _____ (something that you worry about)

I cry _____ (something that makes you sad)

I am _____ (the first line of the poem repeated)

_____

I understand _____ (something that you are certain is true)

I say _____ (something that you believe in)

I dream _____ (something that you would like to be true)

I try _____ (how you are making an effort)

I hope _____ (something that is not an object that you hope for)

I am _____ (repeat the first line of the poem)

Example of "I AM FROM"

I AM FROM

I am from the dark, cool forest, where I hide under the fallen bows of the cedar tree like a scared child, peeking out to see if the world is safe today.

I am from the mountain stream and it's cool, icy water that runs down into the old metal pipe into the gat-so-days.

I am from the wild blackberries and the sour grass that grow on the side of the hill.

I am from the Berry's and the Tahlee's and the Kolbs. I am from Springfrog and Prettyman and Nancy and Aggie and Dutch and Elizabeth.

I am from the Red, the White and the Black, and these are the colors that I wear to honor them when I dance.

I am from the patience of my elders and the temper of my youth.

I am from the stories of rabbit and the heartbeat of the drum and the warm smell of the white oak fire.

I am from the old trunk in my grandmother's bedroom.

I am from frog kerchiefs and corn stalk dolls and beading looms.

I am from chocolate gravy and from fry bread.

I am from the secret night boats of the Antibaptist in Germany, from the long skirts of a freedwoman in Oklahoma and from the little girl who walked the Trail of Those Who Cried.

I am the child who hears a different drum.

I am a person who thinks with the heart.

I am a bead in the story belt of my family.

Example of "I AM FROM"

I AM FROM

I am from that big red backpack that I take when I am moved to a new foster home and from the endless houses that I will never call home.

I am from the one foster home that I thought was my permanent home, and the smell of my very own horse in the pasture, and from apple pie cooling on the top of the oven.

I am from the corn that I helped to grow beside the pasture, so tall and green and sweet, and I am from the tradition of moving me because the people that were going to adopt me, were finally able to get pregnant and have a baby "of their own".

I am from no one, and I have no one, and I bear the name of a family that I will never see, but that is okay with me because they are not healthy.

I am from the tendency to keep my backpack under my bed, where I can get it packed fast when my foster families decide that it is time for me to leave.

I am from the distant memory of my grandmother telling me that she loved me, but then she died, and I am from the recent memory of my foster parents telling me that they loved me, but then I wasn't wanted anymore.

I am from trying to do my best in school and at home and making sure that I was valued, and never having it be enough to be adopted.

I am from the Oregon coast, where my bio-parents were born, and where all of my foster families all liked clam chowder, and so did I, but now it makes me sad.

I am from no family in particular, but I am from families that had a kind heart and took in a little kid that was never good enough for them to belong to them.

I am from sadness, but someday I think that will change.

But until then, I am still from the big red backpack under my bed.

Example of "I AM"

I AM

I am getting better and I try to be honest
I wonder what's going to happen next
I hear a music channel
I want myself back
I am getting better and I try to be honest

I pretend to be in control
I feel confused
I touch tranquility
I worry about losing touch with everything
I cry about what people do
I am getting better and I try to be honest

I understand things can be good
I say pay attention to everything
I dream that people will get along
I try by paying attention to things everyday
I hope for peace
I am getting better and I try to be honest

Example of "I AM"

I AM

I am kind and I care about people

I wonder about pretty much everything

I hear people talking at school

I want to be normal

I am kind and I care about people

———————————

I pretend that I am happy

I feel scared of people, but I don't know why

I worry that people will try to talk to me

I cry when people don't talk to me

I am kind and I care about people

———————————

I understand that I have social anxiety

I say I can get over this

I dream that I am over this

I try to push myself a little every week

I hope that people can see who I really am

I am kind and I care about people

Group #1

Pre-Group and Post-Group

On a scale of 1 - 5, how would you rate your average level of (circle one).

	N/A	A little		Medium		A lot
Social Anxiety (comfort around others)	0	1	2	3	4	5
Impulsivity (thinking before you act)	0	1	2	3	4	5
Positive Mood (happiness, joy)	0	1	2	3	4	5
Negative Mood (anger, sadness)	0	1	2	3	4	5
Frustration	0	1	2	3	4	5
Stress	0	1	2	3	4	5
Focus	0	1	2	3	4	5
Personal Worth	0	1	2	3	4	5
Confidence	0	1	2	3	4	5
Negotiation Skills	0	1	2	3	4	5

Why do you think this group will be therapeutic for you?
_____

What do you hope to gain from this group?
_____

QUESTION FORM

GROUP MEMBER _____   DATE _____

WHAT IF YOU HAD A CHANCE TO BE SOMEONE OR SOMETHING ELSE? WOULD YOU DO IT? WOULD YOU STILL MAKE THE SAME CHOICES? HOW DO YOU KNOW?

_____

_____

_____

QUESTION FORM

GROUP MEMBER _____   DATE _____

HOW ARE YOU AND YOUR CHARACTER SIMILAR? HOW ARE YOU AND YOUR CHARACTER DIFFERENT?

_____

_____

_____

QUESTION FORM

GROUP MEMBER _____   DATE _____

TODAY YOUR COMPANY FACED A SISIUTL AND HAD TO TELL IT YOUR WORTH. WHAT MAKES "WORTH" IN A PERSON? WHAT MAKES YOU WORTHY?

_____

_____

_____

QUESTION FORM

GROUP MEMBER _____   DATE _____

THIS IS A FUN GROUP, BUT IT IS ALSO MEANT TO BE THERAPEUTIC. WHY DO YOU THINK THIS GROUP IS THERAPY FOR YOU?

_____

_____

_____

QUESTION FORM

GROUP MEMBER _____ DATE _____

WHAT HAVE YOU LEARNED ABOUT YOURSELF FROM THIS GROUP?

_____

_____

_____

QUESTION FORM

GROUP MEMBER _____   DATE _____

WHAT WAS THE BEST THING ABOUT TODAY'S GROUP?

_____

_____

_____

QUESTION FORM

GROUP MEMBER _____   DATE _____

WHAT DECISION WERE YOU PROUD OF TODAY IN THE GROUP?

_____

_____

_____

QUESTION FORM

GROUP MEMBER _____   DATE _____

WHAT WAS THE BEST DECISION THAT YOU MADE IN TODAY'S GROUP? DO YOU THINK THAT DECISIONS THAT YOU MAKE IN THE GROUP CAN HELP YOU OUTSIDE THE GROUP?

_____

_____

_____

QUESTION FORM

GROUP MEMBER _____   DATE _____

WHAT HAVE YOU LEARNED ABOUT YOURSELF DURING THIS GROUP?
_____

_____

_____

"People were telling me that I can't use Dungeons & Dragons in real life, but I totally can. Especially the humor. When I saw some kids in the gym that were known for bullying, I raised my arms and turned to the kids that I was with and I said, 'I cast detect evil…. and they laughed with me. That felt pretty good." ~ Half Elf Wizard – Age 13

References

Adams, Aubrie S. (2013) "Needs Met Through Role-Playing Games: A Fantasy Theme Analysis of Dungeons & Dragons," Kaleidoscope: A Graduate Journal of Qualitative Communication Research: Vol. 12, Article 6.

Blackmon, Wayne D. (1994). Dungeons & Dragons: The Use of a Fantasy Game in the Psychotherapeutic Treatment of a Young Adult. American Journal of Psychotherapy, 48 (4), Fall, 624-632.

Gilsdorf, Ethan. "Dungeons & Dragons, 40 Years Old, Makes You A Better Person." *Psychology Today* 1 Feb. 2014. Print.

Harrison, G. E., & Van Haneghan, J. P. (2011). The Gifted and the Shadow of the Night: Dabrowski's Overexcitabilities and Their Correlation to Insomnia, Death Anxiety, and Fear of the Unknown. Journal for the Education of the Gifted, 34(4), 669-697

John Hughes (1988). *Therapy is Fantasy: Roleplaying, Healing and the Construction of Symbolic Order*. Paper presented in Anthropology IV Honours, Medical Anthropology Seminar, Dr. Margo Lyon, Dept. of Prehistory & Anthropology, Australian National University. Retrieved June 13, 2016, from the World Wide Web:http://www.rpgstudies.net/hughes/therapy_is_fantasy.html

Webb, James T. and Latimer, Diane. "ADHD and Children Who Are Gifted". ERIC Digest #522, (1993).

Wizards of the Coast. (2004). Thirty years of adventure: A celebration of Dungeons & Dragons. Renton, WA: Author

"People tell me that I'm a 'natural born leader', but I never believed it. I just thought that was something that adults said to kids to be nice, but when I started in the D&D group, I started to see how it was true. I really was the natural leader of the group. I thought that at first it was because I was good at the game, but then I started thinking about it, and I noticed that I make really good decisions. I guess I do that in my real life too…. I just never noticed before. Knowing that… Being able to see that… That has really helped lift my depression. I feel better about myself. I guess I'm sort of a real life wizard!" ~ Gnome Wizard (age 17)

"The best heroes aren't the ones that started off doing amazing things. The best heroes are the ones that started off like you and me, and they became heroes when they had to." ~ Halfling Cleric, age 12

Links to an interview with Ryan and Bev and their co-worker Deanna during a Comi-Con Panel.

https://www.youtube.com/watch?v=TVvT_EakokU&t=162s

https://www.youtube.com/watch?v=8ArrH3S4UqE

Made in the USA
Lexington, KY
11 November 2019